Your Success Experience

Love The Life You Live

Experience Your Success

Patrick Lowe D.C.

Your Success Experience

Love The Life You Live, Experience Your Success!

Patrick R. Lowe, D.C.

Added Value Publishing
10306 Shelbyville Rd, Louisville KY 40223
Printed in the United States of America

Library of Congress Cataloging-in-Publication Data

Lowe, Patrick R.
  Your Success Experience : Love the life you live, experience your success/ Patrick Lowe
ISBN 0-9799124-0-7
ISBN 13: 978-0-9799124-0-5

Excerpt and paraphrase from "Secrets of the Millionaire Mind" on pg 46&47 ©2005, Harv Eker, Reprinted by permission of HarperCollins Publishers

Excerpt from Harvard Business Review article "The Ethical Mind" by Howard Gardner on page28, Reprinted by permission of Harvard Business School Publishing

(Permissions Continued at back of book)

Your Success Experience

Love The Life You Live, Experience Your Success!

Patrick R. Lowe, D.C.

Dedicated to my wonderful wife, Darlene. Without you, none of this would be possible or have the deep meaning that you teach me.

And our children, Alexander, Spencer, Caleb, and Savannah. The Irish proverb says, "You must do your own growing, no matter how tall your dad is." It is my hope that this book will help you avoid some of the growing pains of life and move to a higher level of Success Experience on your own.

Special Thank you to several people who made this book possible. Amy Hoemeke is a constant positive encourager. Several encouragers read every word several times: Amy Hoemeke, Mary Heady, Denise Gerzonick, Betty Hundley, MaryRuth Vangundy, Ryan Bowman, Renee Pendleton. The people who believe an idea is never too big or impossible. THANK YOU!

Contents

Your Success Experience

Love The Life You Live, Experience Your Success!

Patrick R. Lowe, D.C.

This book is written for ONE person. One person in a million who will not only read the words on the page but also will learn it and apply its teachings, one person in a million who will teach its secrets to others, one person in a million who will grow from it. Are you one in a million? If so, this book is for YOU!

This book is not for the person who reads without doing, who analyzes but never applies. It is written for doers, people of action.

Throughout this book, we will look at how people think, some specific entertaining stories about our thought processes at certain times in our lives. We will explore ways to draw more of the Success Experiences you want into your life. I make fun of how I have thought at certain times in my life. Some of the stories will give you an "aha" experience, others may offend you initially. Think about why it offends you.

Chapter 1

The Success Experience

"Every one of us has his own vocation or mission in life….Thus he cannot be replaced or his life repeated." Viktor Frankl

What is success?

What is the purpose behind our work? This elusive thing called Success. Clichés like "what you consider success is up to you," "Mother Teresa was a success but didn't have a penny to her name," and "Donald Trump is successful, right?" all seem irreconcilable at times. How do you bring together a pious nun and a billionaire in one all-encompassing definition of Success? Yet generic answers like "what success is, is up to you" seem like a great big steaming load of doo doo. I do not believe that people work for money, save money, spend money, or even give away money. We work, save, spend, and give away money for the experience, our Success Experience!

Your Success Experience

Love The Life You Live, Experience Your Success!

Patrick R. Lowe, D.C.

A mother takes pictures of her kids in the school play. A hunter pays hundreds of dollars to mount his trophies and hangs them in his living room. A golfer frames his scorecard showing a hole in one. Ask them why, and they all say that they like to remember the day. They want to relive the experience, "who was there with them," and many other details of the day. It is not about a picture; a picture of someone else's kid in a different play would not do. It is not about a hunter's trophy. (If you find one in a yard sale, his wife is giving it away.) It's not about a scorecard showing a hole in one. It is about remembering and reliving an experience, a "Success Experience."

> **We work, save, spend, and give away money for the experience, our Success Experience!**

My children learned this at an early age. When they were two or three years old, they would be happy to get a trophy for nothing. By the time they were four or five, they only wanted a trophy they had earned and that was associated with an experience. They had learned that the experience gives the trophy value.

Your Success Experience

Love The Life You Live, Experience Your Success!

Patrick R. Lowe, D.C.

We all have millions of "Success Experiences" in our lifetimes. Yet we overlook many of them with a comparison to what we think someone else has achieved. We even categorize things as failures because they are not our "big goal."

> **The most miserable people on the planet are focusing on *having* instead of *experiencing*.**

Success is not a place. It is not a scavenger hunt where the one who gets the most things on the list wins. It is not even about having a lot of money. All of these things can be Success Experiences. They go toward your accumulation of life experiences. The warm fuzzy feeling of security you get when you look at your growing savings account. The feeling of pride you get when you get a new car. The feeling you get from giving to someone less fortunate, your church, or favorite charity.

The vacation you want: an experience.

The TV show you are watching: an experience.

The drive to work: an experience.

Your Success Experience

Love The Life You Live, Experience Your Success!

Patrick R. Lowe, D.C.

The job you have, the spouse you spend time with, the kids you play with, the neighborhood you live in, the bed you go to sleep in, and even the flavor and brand of the toothpaste you use in the morning: all experiences and all based on what you like to experience.

Some of the most miserable people on the planet are focusing on having instead of experiencing.

If it is something you like, something you have achieved, then it is part of your Success Experience! You have probably invested some time, some money, and/or energy into getting it.

If an experience brings you joy, it is a part of your Success Experience.

Success-full

Life is a series of Success Experiences. Being success-full (no, it is not a typo) is accumulating more Success Experiences than non-Success Experiences. It means a winning scorecard. The opposite of successful is not failure; it is unsuccessful. The difference between successful and unsuccessful can be as little as 2%. If an experience shows 49% success, you may

Your Success Experience

Love The Life You Live, Experience Your Success!

Patrick R. Lowe, D.C.

write it down as an unsuccessful experience. If it shows 51% success, put it in as success-full. For a large part, we are all success-full; however, we choose to focus on a few negative details of an experience and write it in as being an unsuccessful experience.

> "Many of life's failures are men who did not realize how close they were to success when they gave up."
>
> **Thomas Edison**

Getting to work in the morning is a Success Experience, being there on time is even better; having an opportunity to go to work is also a success. I have seen people write off the entire morning because someone cut them off in traffic on the way to work. They give that one negative experience more weight than 50 positive experiences, and remember the day as being "unsuccess-full."

9

Failure Experiences are part of Success Experiences

"Many of life's failures are men who did not realize how close they were to success when they gave up." Thomas Edison

It would be unrealistic to say that failures do not occur. Failures can be painful and leave you wondering what is going to happen next. Where do we go from here?

The big question is how much failure can you handle? Which of these events would make you want to quit? Which ones would actually cause you to quit? If you had:

1. Lost your new restaurant in a fire, rebuilt, and then worked it for several years. Then at age 66 had to sell your restaurant, finding yourself with nothing to show for years of hard work?

2. Worked for years to build a huge business, only to have it taken over in a hostile takeover?

3. Started five different businesses and lost all of them?

4. Blown up a building because of your error?

5. Lost both of your brothers in a plane crash, bounced back, and built a second restaurant only to have it destroyed by fire. What if, within weeks of the fire, you

10

were diagnosed with a potentially life-threatening problem requiring two surgeries?

What would you do? Would you quit, hide in a corner?

> **"Every failure brings with it the seed of an equivalent success."**
>
> Napoleon Hill

The first scenario is the life of Colonel Harlan Sanders. By 1937, Colonel Harlan Sanders had built a restaurant that seated 142 people. Two years later a fire destroyed his work. He rebuilt and enjoyed great success until a new highway opened, bypassing his restaurant. He sold his restaurant and after paying his outstanding bills, had to live on Social Security, $105 per month.

Did he quit? No, at age 62, he started selling his secret recipe to restaurant owners.

He drove from town to town, cooking chicken for them. They would agree to pay him 5 cents for each bucket of chicken they sold. When he was 74, he sold his franchise business for $2 million and continued to be the spokesman for the company. [1]

The second scenario is Steve Wynn's story. Mr. Wynn started his casino career at the Golden Nugget. He is credited with building the "New Las Vegas." After building the Mirage, Treasure Island, and the Bellagio, a hostile takeover forced him out of the company. He recently opened the Wynn Hotel and Casino in Las Vegas. He immediately moved on to open another Wynn Casino and Resort in Macau, China. He continues designing beautiful casinos and resorts, in spite of an inherited eye disease. [2]

The third scenario refers to Napoleon Hill. Napoleon spent time with Andrew Carnegie, the wealthiest man on the planet at the time. He interviewed other great leaders like Henry Ford, Thomas Edison, and John D. Rockefeller. He even worked with Presidents Franklin D. Roosevelt and William Howard Taft. He wrote one of the best self-help books of all time, *Think and Grow Rich.* He started several companies, all of which eventually failed. He never quit. [3]

The fourth scenario is Jack Welch's story. Jack retired as one of the highest paid executives in US history. He had turned a successful company, General Electric, into one of the top ten companies in the country. He is an engineer by trade. For his first management assignment, he was in charge of a chemical plant that mixed volatile chemicals. An unexpected spark ignited the chemicals, blowing the roof off the plant. As the leader, it was his responsibility. Fortunately, no one was seriously hurt. Some would perceive that to be failure and quit. Jack took responsibility and made a huge impact on his company over the course of his career. [4]

The final scenario is Truett Cathy's story. He is the founder of Chick-fil-A, who suffered many losses. His two brothers were also his business partners in a restaurant. A plane crash claimed the live of both of his brothers. Truett managed to keep the restaurant going and even added a second restaurant.

> "Failure is simply a price we pay to achieve success."
>
> John Maxwell

A fire destroyed the second restaurant. Within weeks of the fire, he was diagnosed with colon polyps. His treatment involved surgery and months of recovery. It was during this time that the Chick-fil-A concept began.

Now, Chick-Fil-A is one of the fastest growing privately owned restaurant chain in America. He apparently didn't quit. He is a true inspiration. His goal is to continue mentoring the young people who work for his restaurants. [5]

Your Success Experience

Love The Life You Live, Experience Your Success!

Patrick R. Lowe, D.C.

Failure experiences are experiences; they are events, not people. Too often, people associate failure experiences with themselves and accept it as part of their identity. I am a failure, he is a failure, she is a failure. Failure is an event. John Maxwell states, "Failure is simply a price we pay to achieve success." [6]

> "Sometimes adversity is what you need to face in order to become successful."
>
> Zig Ziglar

"Every failure brings with it the seed of an equivalent success." Napoleon Hill

Do you think that Colonel Sanders would have started his franchise business if his restaurant had continued to be successful? Probably not, there was nothing to move him out of his comfort zone. Once he felt the pressure of living on $105 per month, he was motivated to create the great chicken empire by the failure of his restaurant. Because of his unsuccessful experience, he was able to give a lot more to his community, his country, and his family. Zig Ziglar says, "Sometimes adversity is what you need to face in order to become successful." [7] The same is true of all of the other great people listed above. Many authors calls it "Failing

Forward." Use failures to create even larger Success Experiences.

What is in your bank?

No, I do not mean your financial status. I am referring to something more important than that. Many years from now, when you are looking back over your life, what memories will you have created and stored into your memory bank? Your bank only holds a certain number of deposits.

Throughout our lives, we have Success Experiences. We also have our share of non-Success Experiences. We choose which experiences to place in our memory banks. It is not always a conscious decision; it is a decision of repetition. The more times we tell a story, good or bad, the bigger it becomes in our memory bank.

Then when we need to call up a memory or story to tell, we will grab the largest applicable deposit item from the past from our long-term investments.

When something unfortunate happens to you and you tell everyone you meet about it, it will become a long-term investment. You are rehearsing the story about how bad your life is.

Ironically, when a Success Experience occurs we only tell a few people. We are raised to be humble and not brag. Therefore, it goes into our memory bank as a small deposit item.

Then, when you are talking to friends many years from now and a similar subject comes up, what story will come to mind? The one you have rehearsed, the one you have practiced delivering, and every detail comes flowing back, as if it were a part that you memorized for a school play. Is it any wonder that some people are unhappy?

> **The more times we tell a story, good or bad, the bigger it becomes in our memory bank.**

Be aware of what stories you tell and retell. While talking about negative experiences helps relieve stress, it also imbeds them in your memory bank. Telling and retelling a story feeds the experience and puts it into your permanent memory bank, especially if it is charged with emotion.

Every time you tell a story, you remember more small details and put it in your bank to pull out when the need arises.

> **Confidence is the natural dividend paid on accounts with a positive balance.**

Confidence is the natural dividend paid on accounts with a positive balance. The more positive stories you add to your memory bank, the higher your dividends, Confidence.

Fear and doubt are the natural penalties charged for a memory bank filled with negative stories.

What are you putting in your bank? In chapter 7, we will talk about techniques to increase your positive deposits.

Your ideal Success Experiences

This is not a tough intellectual process. It does not require a lot of thought. You do not have to go to a mountain in isolation or spend a year in Tibet with monks to figure it out. It is as easy as answering two questions.

#1 If money were not a consideration, what would you spend most of your time doing?

#2 What would you LOVE to do or invest a lot of time and resources in doing on a regular basis?

Success changes

Your Success Experience changes as you have other experiences, as you age, as you go through different phases of life. This is exactly why people almost never feel fully successful. Success is not a destination. It is a lifelong process. When I was 17, my goal was to earn a little money and to go to college. Then my goal changed to actually staying in school after my first quarter. After a couple of quarters with reasonable grades, I considered getting through undergraduate school to be success. While in college, I worked full time. I developed the dream of marrying my high school sweetheart, Darlene. I knew I would be successful when I could buy a house and get married. I bought my first house

> **Success is not a destination. It is a lifelong process.**

Your Success Experience

Love The Life You Live, Experience Your Success!

Patrick R. Lowe, D.C.

for $22,000 in 1992 and married the love of my life. What a success!

At the time, I was working making $17,000 per year. I considered that a lot of money, at that time. One of my goals was to make $20,000 per year. I am glad that Success changes as we grow and change.

Moving beyond your Success Experiences

"If what you did yesterday, still looks pretty big to you, then you haven't done enough today." Earle Wilson [8]

After each Success Experience, another phase of life comes up, another opportunity comes into view. Count each Success Experience as an achievement and look forward to the next one. It is important to move forward looking for the next one.

Many football teams have a 24-hour rule. When the team wins, players can talk and celebrate the win for 24 hours. After that, they have to move on to prepare for the next game. Run their patterns, lift their weights, and get back into training. Players know that to have a winning season, they have to prepare for the next challenge. Next week's opponent is coming soon; achieving your next Success Experience (winning the game) depends on preparing for it today.

Identifying your Success Experiences

Where do you get your Success Experience fix? We all crave them, and we get them. Are you getting the experiences you want out of life?

John complains that he never has any money in the bank. Why is that? It could be that John gets his daily Success Experiences from something other than working. It could be that he gets his Success Experiences from spending money. It could even be that John works, makes lots of money, but gets his Success Experiences from giving away a lot of money.

Identify what makes it a Success Experience for you.

If you get your Success Experience from something other than working, where do you get it? Are you a sports junkie? Is your idea of success to not work or have anything to do?

Do new fancy clothes make you feel successful? They do me. Think about where that feeling started. Is it a "hand-me-down" feeling that you just accepted from your parents or friends, or is it a feeling that supports your overall success?

Other people get their "fix" only from saving. Having money in the bank only and never spending or giving. Where does this come from? Does it stem from feelings of fear, fear of never having enough?

Think back about your most memorable Success Experiences. What made them GREAT? Were they gifts from someone else? Did you earn them? My most gratifying Success Experiences come from activities where I have invested time and energy. I enjoy earning money for the family vacation, spending time planning and thinking about it, even dreaming about it for weeks. Most of all I enjoy sharing the experience with other people, my family.

The question is, "HOW CAN I GET MORE ?"

All of the Success Experiences of your life will come from your head and your heart and the decisions you make. We all want more Success Experiences. We have big goals and enjoy the little Success Experiences.

In the rest of this book, we will look at how highly successful people think, feel, decide, and act. We will also look at what holds people back. In chapter 7, we will talk about how small daily improvements will help you achieve all of the "Success Experiences" you desire. We will challenge your thoughts, reprogram your mind, and sell you to you.

It's the LAW!

Conscious Awareness

I recently bought a new luxury car. When we visited the Lexus dealership, we fell in love with a small SUV that would easily transport my family of six. We were amazed at all of the amenities. The leather seats, the heated seats, even the color. The salesman showed a few of the features but let us discover the rest of it ourselves. What an experience! He knew that if he got us into the car and let us have the experience of finding the cool amenities, we would sell ourselves on the car. He was always available to answer questions but did little talking otherwise. "Wow, look at this, the seats are heated, the wipers come on automatically, and, even better, dual climate control. You are ALWAYS cold!" After driving and buying the car, I was convinced that we had a rare vehicle indeed. Not many other people would have this, right?

Now that we had one, I started to notice how many of these Lexus SUVs are driven.

Your Success Experience

Love The Life You Live, Experience Your Success!

Patrick R. Lowe, D.C.

Were there actually more sales of this model after I bought one? Of course not. I had activated the recognition center in my brain to recognize other Lexus SUV's, especially ones just like we had bought.

That is conscious awareness. Because I was conscious of the cars, I became aware of all of them around me.

Try this: Look at this symbol, λ think about it, stare at it for 60 seconds, and think about how it makes you feel. It seems unique, doesn't it? Now that you have given it a little attention, you will begin to recognize symbols like it around you in seemingly mundane places. It may be in your floor tiles or engraved in a stone. It may show up on a map.

How do we apply this to success? Spend some time developing your conscious awareness of Success Experiences, experiences you want.

If Napoleon Hill was right when he said, "What you think about expands," why not think about things that we want to expand? We want to expand our vision, our actions, and our list of Success Experiences.

Chapter 2

Money, Success and Significance

What is most important for success?

What is the most important part of your Success Experience? Is it your money, your health, loving relationships, productive work? What is the most important part of your Success Experience?

Match the columns for how long you can live without each:

Oxygen   4 days

Food   4 seconds

Nerve Supply   4 minutes

Water   40 days

Your Success Experience

Love The Life You Live, Experience Your Success!

Patrick R. Lowe, D.C.

The Answer: You can live without food for 40 days, Water for 4 days, Oxygen for 4 minutes, and Nerve Supply for only 4 seconds.

Nerve supply (communication from your brain to your body) is the most important. You can only live 4 seconds without it, but after 4 minutes without oxygen, the nerve supply does not matter much. You have to have both things present.

> **"Money isn't the most important thing in life, but it's reasonably close to oxygen."**
>
> Zig Ziglar

The same applies when people say things like "Money isn't the most important thing" or "Money isn't as important as Love" or "My health is more important than money." They are completely different things, and each one works with the other to make for a healthy person.

Food is the least important item on the list. However, we spend more time thinking about what to eat for dinner than anything else on the list.

It is important to understand how all of these things are part of your Success Experiences. They are all very important to long-term success.

Unsuccessful people habitually justify their lack of money: "No one needs that much money," "Money is not the most important thing," "He must have done something illegal to get all of that," "The rich get richer, the poor get poorer."

Zig Ziglar says, "Money isn't the most important thing in life, but it's reasonably close to oxygen on the 'gotta have it' scale."

Substitute the word *oxygen* for *money:* "No one needs that much oxygen." "He must have done something illegal to suck that much air," "The rich breathe easy, and the poor turn blue."

In reality, our world has a sufficient supply of oxygen and money. There is an abundance of both. Both are recycled. Our bodies use oxygen and produce carbon dioxide, plants recycle it back to oxygen. People earn money and spend money. Both oxygen and money are in a cycle. There is not a shortage of either.

Are you working under water?

Money is an important aspect of success for most people. It gives us opportunities that just are not available without it.

Your Success Experience

Love The Life You Live, Experience Your Success!

Patrick R. Lowe, D.C.

Inadequate supply of money is like living underwater with a small air tank. Yes, you can get by with a little oxygen, but you cannot do very much. You cannot run or swim very hard; you will run out of oxygen. You cannot give much away to help others. You need it all. Your whole life becomes about acquiring more oxygen so that you have enough to last you through your retirement. That is not success.

If you do not believe that oxygen is important, try working underwater. Nerve supply is more important than oxygen, but you cannot do much without both.

Health, loving relationships, money, spiritual growth, and productive work all are part of your greatest Success Experience: YOUR LIFE! At the end of your life, you will reflect on all of these. Your life is your greatest Success Experience!

How do you think and feel about money?

In many lectures, I have ask, "Does Money Change People?" Some people answer yes, others say no. I explain that money is a great big magnifying glass. It makes you more of what you already are.

That is an understatement. Money is a high-powered microscope. You can take a piece of a leaf or a bug, look at it under a high-powered microscope and see exactly its makeup. Money has the same effect. Unsuccessful people will complain that money covers up a lot of wrongdoing. In many ways, it exposes things about you.

Harvard Business Review published a study on business ethics in 2007, written by Howard Gardner:

"A study conducted by Duke University recently found that 56% of students in the United States pursuing a master's degree in business administration admit to cheating... A study we [Harvard Business Review] published in 2004 found that although young professionals declare an understanding and a desire to do good work, they felt that they had to succeed by whatever means. When they had made their mark, they told us, they would then become exemplary workers." [9]

If you are unethical as a student, you are likely to be unethical as a businessperson. If you are a nice, honest, giving person when you are broke, you are very likely to be a nice, honest, giving person when you have money. If you are an ass when you are broke, you are likely to be a GREAT BIG ASS when you have money.

How are people with money portrayed on TV and movies?

Many story lines show people with money as the bad guy. You will notice a slant against money on sitcoms and dramas. Who is often the bad guy? Who is the guy shown cheating on his wife with problem children and a host of other personal problems? The Rich Guy!

Do your own research on the shows. How many episodes have this theme? How many episodes of your favorite drama portray a conflict between someone with money and someone without money? They show the wealthy person as snobbish, unfriendly, and generally antisocial. The more money they have, the more dislikable they make them.

Why? It is a popular idea.

If you want more money in your life, turn off the TV.

Contribution and significance

Contribution: Your big idea, your big Success Experience, what does it do for other people?

In his book *Rich Dad, Poor Dad,* Robert Kiyosaki states, "The rich don't work for money." [10] That is true, and if you don't spend much time around wealthy people, you may assume that they sit at the country club all day, every day, and do absolutely nothing. What I have found is quite different. No, they do not work for money.
They work for significance.

Robert Kiyosaki is rich, but he still writes books, and he travels to lecture. Each of these things requires a lot of time and energy. Why? He could easily do absolutely nothing, live out his life, and never have to worry about money. He does it for a deeper reason, a different type of Success Experience.

> **"The rich don't work for money"**
>
> Robert Kiyosaki

In his book *Half Time,* author Bob Buford talks about a paradigm shift that people go through in their lives. He says the first half of your work life is often dedicated toward becoming successful in the business or trade of your choice. The second half of your career life is increasingly becoming about significance. What can I do to make a significant impact or contribution to others? It is not about retiring just to a life of ease and being served; it is about purpose and helping others. [11]

It is a change in their Success Experience! Success comes from being more, not just earning more. Our population as a whole is aging. We are finding a larger shift toward this type of Success Experience.

> **"We make a living from what we get; we make a life from what we give."**
>
> Winston Churchill [21]

I have been fortunate lately to be able to talk with top executives of Fortune 500 companies. One of the overriding themes that come out is their corporate Success Experience. I have never worked in a large corporation, so my perspective is definitely from the outside in. Yet to talk with these people over dinner you find that they are most excited, most animated when talking about what their company does to make the world a better place and how they personally contribute to the company's success in doing so! They have already identified that their personal Success Experiences and corporate Success

Your Success Experience

Love The Life You Live, Experience Your Success!

Patrick R. Lowe, D.C.

Experiences all come from contributing, adding value to the community, the country, and the world.

There are several ways to contribute to others. Let's use our example of Mother Teresa and Donald Trump. Mother Teresa made a huge contribution to the people of Calcutta and inspired the world.

On the other hand we have Donald Trump. He has made billions of dollars; has he contributed to others? I ask this question when I speak, and the most common answer is, "I don't know how much he gives to charity." I do not know either; that is off the point. He has contributed to the lives and Success Experiences of others by providing jobs, jobs for construction workers, jobs for clerical personnel, and jobs for the electric company and the water company. His projects dump billions of dollars into the economy, pay taxes for roads, build hospitals, and, through their jobs, provide others the Success Experiences of earning, saving, and giving money to charity.

Which is more successful? If you base success on their contributions to others, then both are highly successful.

The truth about money and your Success Experiences

Money plays an important role in most of our Success Experiences. Mother Teresa did not walk to Calcutta. The Catholic Church helped fund her ministry. She actively worked and inspired people to give money to help others, she encouraged people to give money, time and love.

> **Money is a tool that provides us with more opportunities, opportunities to give, to help, to contribute.**

Money is a part of the whole picture. Two of our good friends decided that they wanted to adopt an orphan girl from China. China has very strict laws,designed to slow their population growth. A lot of baby girls are orphaned, neglected or even allowed to die. Still, process to adopt one of these children and bring them to the States costs several thousand dollars.

Another family, the Gerzonicks, wanted to go with their church on a mission trip to Ghana, in Africa. The trip, the food, the experience depended on their ability to raise the money for their trip. Money is a tool that provides us with opportunities, opportunities to give, to help, and to contribute to the lives of others.

Chapter 3

The Psychology of Change

Recalibrating our thoughts, feelings, decisions and actions to allow success

"Many people die at age twenty one but are not buried until age sixty five." Les Brown [12]

Most people run their lives on autopilot. Their goal in life is to be comfortable and undisturbed. They only change when things "look good enough or hurt bad enough." Unfortunately, the "hurt bad enough" is the main motivator for many people. Even then, they change just enough to get from "pain" to "no pain." They never grow much because their goal is to be "comfortable," have no pain, and get through life. I hereby guarantee that you will get through your life, until it ends. Now let's move on.

As a student pilot, I learned that autopilot has limited functions. Autopilot is a computer where you put in a heading, a distance, and you can even tell it when to turn the plane. The ability of autopilot to get you to your destination depends on your ability to calculate the correct flight path and distance. It cannot take off or land the plane. It cannot communicate with the tower or check weather conditions. It cannot make necessary changes based on winds, weather, or other unexpected events. Contrary to popular belief, autopilot does not allow you to sleep walk your way through a flight. Autopilot helps control altitude, speed, and heading. It helps the pilot fly the plane, but it is only a tool. The pilot is in control.

In order to change your altitude, you have to reset your autopilot.

The goal is to get your autopilot to lead you in the right direction, toward your goals. Our hometown, like many cities, sponsors a couple of events a year for runners. The events start with a short race, a longer race a few weeks later, and end the series with a marathon or a mini-marathon. The second year I started training for the races, I discovered that my running autopilot takes over after the first mile. On those mornings when every step felt heavy, when it was rainy or muggy, I would tell myself, "I like to run." Then I would say, "step, step" and set my pace. After the first mile, my running autopilot would take over and I would finish my run without thinking about the pace or the steps. I could focus on other things, the course, the dog that ran out to greet me, and enjoying the scenery.

Running is not a habit; it is a series of choices or decisions. Every choice I made in the direction of my goals, led to the next decision and it was easier. Eventually, my biggest decision was to get out of the door.

The challenge is to get your autopilot to help you reach your goals. Successful people do not rely on it to run their entire lives, they use it as a tool.

Our thoughts, feelings, decisions, and actions set and reset our autopilots.

Thoughts lead to feelings, feeling lead to decisions, decisions lead to actions and all of these create our experiences. If I were to hand you a box and tell you that it contained a present for my nine-year-old son, I have given you a *thought*.

How would you feel about that?

Would you decide to hold the box, to make certain that nothing happened to it? Holding the box is an *action* based on a *decision*. You made this decision based on how you *felt* about the *thought* of a little boys present.

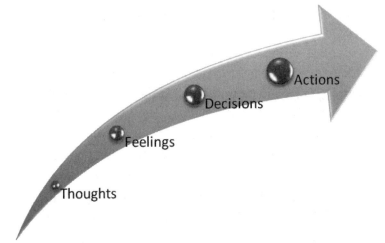

Now, someone else comes up and gives you an additional thought. "Pat's nine-year-old son loves snakes, especially poisonous ones."

Then added, "People carry snakes in boxes like that."

Would the change in *thoughts* change your *feelings* about holding the box? Would the change in feelings change your *decision* about holding the box?

Would you decide to put it down and step away slowly?

Thoughts lead to feelings, feelings in turn lead to decisions, and our decisions lead to actions.

Your Success Experience

Love The Life You Live, Experience Your Success!

Patrick R. Lowe, D.C.

Once you understand the processes, you can use it to change your life.

This process is very specific in its order. Trying to change only your actions, without changing the thoughts and feelings behind it, is like pushing a rope.

When I was in college, I was working on the electricity on our house. One of the last jobs was to thread a piece of wire through a long piece of conduit (the hard tube used to protect electrical wires from damage). The wire is coated with a sticky plastic and was just a little smaller than the conduit. I worked and worked. I pushed it in a short distance and it would stick. I pulled it out and tried again; the wire would twist, get on a bind, and become stuck. The more wire I successfully got in the tube, the more likely it would become stuck. I worked on this part of the project for two days.

A friend came over and saw what I was doing. He said, "Why don't you pull the wire?" He showed me how to drop a line through the conduit, tape it to your wire, and easily pull the wire through. He explained, "Pat, you can't push a rope or a wire."

The same is true when we try to push our actions to change our feelings and thoughts. Like pushing a rope, the harder we push, the more we get stuck in our old ways. It does not work.

What you are thinking and doing today is creating tomorrow's Success Experiences!

"Everything we are is the result of thought." Buddha

At first glance, that seems a little mystical. As we now know, thoughts lead to actions. All of our feelings are the result of thoughts, and our actions are the result of our feelings, so … it is true.

Three different people having exactly the same experience will have completely different ideas about their experience. One considers it a success, the second does not consider it at all, and the third considers it a failure. Why? We filter all of our experiences through our thoughts and emotions.

One of the questions therapists ask their patients is, "How did you feel about that?" They realize that in order to change, you have to identify how you think and feel. Understanding your emotions in a situation allows you to explore other possibilities.

Your Success Experience

Love The Life You Live, Experience Your Success!

Patrick R. Lowe, D.C.

All experiences start with a thought, followed by a feeling, then a decision, and result in an action.

Our thoughts

"The more you know ..."

When TV only offered three channels, *Schoolhouse Rock* aired between Saturday morning cartoons. One of its slogans was "Knowledge is Power." NBC is now sponsoring public service messages called "The more you know...."

> **All Success Experiences are the result of a thought, a feeling, a decision, and an action.**

All of these slogans are based on the idea that information, or knowledge, is all that is necessary to change things. Let's test this theory with a few questions.

1. How often are you supposed to change the filter in your furnace?

2. How often should you change the oil in your car?

3. What is the legal speed limit on a highway?

Your Success Experience

Love The Life You Live, Experience Your Success!

Patrick R. Lowe, D.C.

You probably know that you should change your furnace filter once a month, change your oil once every 90 days or 3,000 miles, and what the speed limit is in your state. How many of these do you accomplish regularly? If you knew the answers to one or more of them and do not do it, it shows that knowledge (information) alone is useless, unless you can use it to answer questions on *Jeopardy*.

Information has great value when you understand it and apply it. Speaker and Philosopher Dr. Jay Morgan suggests changing the slogans to "Knowledge in action is Power" or "The more you know and Do." It will take you a lot farther. [13]

Thoughts lead to feelings, feelings lead to decisions, decisions lead to actions, and actions create our Success Experiences.

How do we change our lives, our world?

One of the big mistakes that I have noticed is that people try to change their actions to change their habits. They try to FORCE themselves through sheer will to change their lives, to create Success Experiences by acting in a certain way, only to become frustrated when things do not change.

They often find themselves backsliding.

They are working the equation in the wrong order. You can change the way you act for a short time. Backsliding occurs and old habits re-emerge. When things go wrong, we pull up memories of good feelings associated with the old habits. When we are under stress, we try to recapture the good feelings that we learned with the old habit. We convince ourselves that we are miserable because of the changes we have made. Since we think it and feel it, we go back to our old ways.

How can we be successfully change a habit? It is a three-part process, illustrated here:

1) Change how you think about the habit.

2) Change how you FEEL about the habit.

3) Then and only then will your actions permanently change.

I am a reformed smoker. One of the things I learned when I was quitting is that quitting is hard. It was hard when I tried to change my actions only. There are a lot of "How to" books on the market. These books are GREAT if you are fixing a sink or working on a car. When it comes to changing the way you act or experience success, acting like someone else just does not seem to work. Why? Our actions are the result of our thoughts and feelings. When something goes wrong, we revert to what worked for us in the past.

I started smoking at a very young age. I was 14. I thought that it was so cool. I could picture how cool it would be to be driving in my car at age 16, one hand on the wheel and one with a lit cigarette, the smoke wafting and swirling before it headed out of the window. That was success! My own car, my own smokes, how could the girls resist running over and smothering me with kisses?

> **If you want to change a habit, change how you think and feel about it.**

What you think of as look forward to and plan for is part of your perceived Success Experience.

Do you think that I quit smoking before I was 16? HE_ _ NO! It took until I was 18 to start seeing that it was not cool. I justified my smoking by surrounding myself with other smokers.

If you want to change something in your life, change how you think and feel about it!

Your Success Experience

Love The Life You Live, Experience Your Success!

Patrick R. Lowe, D.C.

I did quit smoking when I entered graduate school. It was not easy. My new friends thought it was "disgusting". The people around me no longer supported my habit. I was attending Chiropractic College, studying natural health care, planning to start my own office after graduation. I realized that my future future wasn't as bright, if I kept this habit. Graduate school changed my thoughts and feelings about smoking. I was able to quit.

> "If you want to change the fruits, you will first have to change the roots."
>
> T. Harve Eker

I once (or twice) found comfort or a Success Experience from eating. This is easy to do when we have phrases in our language to support it: "Eating high off the hog," "Beer budget and a Champagne appetite," and many others.

During graduate school and for the first two years after, my wife and I were thin. We were thin, not by choice, but because we could not afford much food. As time went on, we could afford more so we bought more, ate out more (because we could afford it, and deserved it), and I grew more, and more, and more, a solid 50 pounds more. Notice that eating and eating out were part of my Success Experience. Until I saw a picture of myself with my kids and I was shocked. Other successful people I admired, were not 50 pounds overweight!

So, I changed my Success Experience again! The change in behavior followed the change in feelings and change in thought.

In his book *Secrets of the Millionaire Mind,* Harve Eker says, "If you want to change the fruits, you will first have to change the roots." People spend a lot of time acting in a certain way and waiting for success. Farmers know that if you do not like the fruits that a tree is producing you have

> **"We look for lessons in the actions of great leaders. We should instead be examining what goes on in their heads."**
>
> Roger Martin

change what you are putting on the soil and strengthen the roots of the plant. The roots are your thoughts. [14]

How you think about something relates to how you feel about it. People generally act on feelings. Emotions motivate us. Fear drives us away from harm; Love draws us to each other.

Your Success Experience

Love The Life You Live, Experience Your Success!

Patrick R. Lowe, D.C.

Very few decisions are based solely on logic or knowledge. Psychologists tell us that nearly all decisions are based on emotion. It applies to selling and it applies to changing habits.

Analyzing our own thoughts and patterns is a huge undertaking. We have over 1500 thoughts a minute; most of them are on autopilot. Autopilot runs on previous patterns. Have you ever been driving along, going somewhere near where you work, and missed the turn? Autopilot.

> **"You can't see the picture when you're in the frame."**
>
> Les Brown

Have you ever forgotten your watch, and then looked at your arm 100 times? Autopilot.

Speaker and writer Les Brown says, "You can't see the picture when you're in the frame." It is difficult to get an objective look at ourselves.

Let's look at some self-destructive thought patterns and see what you think.

Sue is trying to lose 25 pounds. She has tried several different times and several different diets. Nothing seemed to work.

She loses 5 pounds very quickly. She tells herself, "I can't wait until I lose all of this weight, then I can eat whatever I want." At the risk of sounding unsympathetic, it was eating whatever she wanted that gave her the extra 25 pounds in the first place!

John had a good job, but he has credit card debt out the Wazoo. He tells himself, "I can't wait until I get these credit cards paid down, then I can buy whatever I want!" HMMMM

Becky has relationship trouble, and says, "I always fall for the _____ guys." Did she trip? Was she unconscious when she agreed to go on a second date with him? No, it was an emotional decision based on the fear of not having anyone.

"We look for lessons in the actions of great leaders. We should instead be examining what goes on in their heads." Roger Martin [15]

Echo, Echo, Echo

Your brain is a huge echo machine. You will notice that most echoes only repeat the last word! People think and say things like "I am going to lose weight!" Their brain echoes Weight,

Your Success Experience

Love The Life You Live, Experience Your Success!

Patrick R. Lowe, D.C.

Weight, Weight, Weight... You know that what they think about expands, so they GAIN weight! Now they are frustrated and think they failed because of their actions, their weakness, or the diet they chose. Their echo machines have sabotaged their emotions.

They decide to "watch what I eat!" Like an obedient echo machine, it echoes eat, eat, eat! Then they feel like they are depriving themselves because they are not eating when they think about it.

How about people who decide to quit smoking; the echo machine says, "Smoking, smoking, smoking, smoking" and they go from ½ pack a day to 1 ½ packs a day.

Once you understand how the echo machine works, you can use it to your benefit. It takes a little effort to change your thought patterns and word patterns. Talk and think about what you want by replacing negative words with positive words.

Replace	With
Don't	Do
Won't	Will
Can't	Yet
If	When

Try	Will
But	And

Omit the words "Wish" and "Should." They are always followed by the word "but."

Change Don't to Do

"I don't want to go to dinner" to "I want to eat in tonight."

Change Won't to Will

"I won't make it in time" to "I will leave earlier next time."

Change Can't to Yet

Change "I can't get into college" to "I haven't gotten into college yet."

Change "They won't let me in" to "I haven't met criteria yet."

Change If to When

Change "If I get my big break, I will be a star" to "When I get my big break, I will be a star."

Change Try to Will

"There is no try, only do" (Yoda). The word "Try" shows a lack of commitment to the outcome.

Change "I will try" to "I will."

<u>But to And</u>

The word "But" makes a liar out everything that comes before it.

"I love your new dress, but…" really means, "I do not love your new dress. I do not even like your new dress."

Change "But" to "And." "I love your hair and your new shoes… (I still hate that dress)."

Our feelings!

"As he thinketh in his heart, so is he." Proverbs 23:7

At first glance, it looks like Solomon, the author, had a typo. I don't know about you, but in my schooling the head think-eth and the heart feel-eth, my eyes see-eth and my ears hear-eth.

It actually shows King Solomon's wisdom and understanding. Written over 3,000 years ago, he knew that thoughts and feelings determine a person's Success Experiences.

How can I change how I feel about something?

Realize many things we feel are choices.

That is right, they are choices. Let's look at anger. Have you ever been angry at someone, gotten through the day, and found yourself talking with them, joking with them, then said, "I forgot that I am angry at you!" If you can forget it, it is a thought. Anger is a thought. Rage on the other hand is a chemically based emotion, where the person often loses control.

Many types of fears and anxiety are also choices based on how we think, fear of public speaking, fear of clowns. The two major types of fears are learned fears and instinctive fears. Learned fears are acquired through our own experiences or through what other people tell us. We call these fears and they do make us uncomfortable. Not everyone has the same learned fears.

Instinctive fears, on the other hand, are hard wired into our brains. Everyone on the planet has the same fear. If you are walking in the woods and come face to face with a tiger or a wolf, the Fear you feel is a chemical emotion! The drive for survival is not a thought; it is an instinct.

Once we know the difference, we realize we can overcome many of our learned fears. We can choose feelings that support our success.

FEAR

The most destructive of emotions is fear. It immobilizes some, paralyzes others, and causes irrational behavior.

Lesson from the dog trainer on Fear

For Christmas this year, we got a Doberman puppy. When she was four moths old, we took her for obedience training.

Before agreeing to train our dog, the trainer did some testing. Testing to see if she was "hand shy," "foot shy," or generally afraid of people. The trainer explained, "A dog that is fearful is much more likely to bite than a dog that is confident."

The same is true for people. The more confident you are, truly confident, the less likely you will lash out at other people. When a fearful person perceives that they are threatened, they react in ways that confident people do not.

53

I have studied martial arts for years. The highest-ranking, best fighters are the least likely to ever need to use their skills. They work to avoid situations that could lead to conflict or threaten others. When confronted, they apologize and work to resolve the conflict peacefully.

Confidence is personal power. Fear destroys confidence.

To build confidence, focus on past Success Experiences and not on failures. Challenge yourself regularly in new ways. Overcome fears and don't make excuses for them.

You will NEVER ALLOW YOURSELF TO BECOME SOMEONE YOU DON'T LIKE!

If you think rich people are snobs, you probably won't become one, you won't build positive relationships with them, and you won't learn how to become rich yourself.

My weight changes at times, based primarily on … well, how much I eat and if I am exercising or not. I was sitting at a restaurant with a friend and said, "I ate too much; I need to cut back and lose some weight." He replied, "I have just the opposite problem, I can't eat enough!" **Don't you just hate people like that?**

I don't, because if I say that I hate that person, I will NEVER BECOME THAT PERSON! You know why he can't get enough to eat? HE RUNS MARATHONS. He ran a local marathon one week and ran the Boston Marathon within 7 days!

I can be that person when I think right and act right to do it! Celebrate other people's successes and you will surely have more of them yourself. Being truly happy for someone else's Success Experience prepares you for yours. It also builds the relationship.

I admire business people who have the financial Success Experiences. I also admire athletes, musicians, and artists. I admire people who are at the top. I most admire those who have reached the top by contributing to the lives of others.

> **A big decision is only a starting point for a series of decisions.**

Decision making

Have you ever made a decision that stood by itself? Every big decision is supported by many little decisions. You decide to go out for dinner (Big Decision). Now you have to decide where to go, what time, how to get there, what to wear, who to invite, what to drink, what to order, do you want desert, and, finally, how to pay. A big decision is only a starting point for a series of decisions.

I have a friend who smokes. She decided to quit and purposely ran out of cigarettes at night so she could start the next day as a nonsmoker. On the way to work, she started to worry that she would have stress and "need a cigarette," so she stopped at the store and bought a pack. A pack contains 20 cigarettes. Did she quit? No, she made 20 little decisions that didn't go along with her big decision to quit smoking. Actually, she made 20 little decisions for each cigarette she smoked and had 20 cigarettes, so she made 400 little decisions.

Are the little decisions you are making today supporting the big decisions you made yesterday?

Making decisions work

Japanese companies are highly respected for their efficiency and their ability to make things happen, once they have made a decision. They approach decision making slightly differently than we do. The call in everyone who will be implementing the decision and get their feedback on the problems, the solutions, the plans, and the potential outcomes of the decision. Then when they are ready to start a project, everyone is on board and understands the process.

I try to utilize this method in my home life as well as with work. Call in the people whom the decision will affect and talk with them about the potential pros and cons.

At our Chiropractic office, we were faced with the challenge of increased health insurance premiums. This year it would be 25%. I called in the people who were on the plan and talked with them about it. I spelled out the increase, how much their portion would increase, and options for reducing the costs. The decision took a lot longer to reach than if I had made it myself. However, using this approach, everyone who is affected puts in his or her ideas. We decided to decrease our benefits and keep down the costs.

It is the difference between doing something **to** someone and doing something **with** someone. People like to have a voice in decisions that affect them. You will uncover possible challenges that you never thought about and will make better decisions. It also shows that you respect their contribution to the outcome.

ACTIONS

> "Until a decision has degenerated into work and the stage of actual execution, for all intents and purposes, no decision has been made."
>
> Peter Drucker

Our actions are the result of our thoughts, our feelings, and our decisions.

"Until a decision has degenerated into work and reaches the stage of actual execution, for all intents and purposes, no decision has been made." Peter Drucker [16]

As a reformed smoker, I am amazed at how I thought and acted about smoking. If there was a room full of smokers who were told that a tornado was heading toward their house, they will each light up as many cigarettes as they can find. "Oh my, I'm going to die" (Puff, puff, puff). "This is so stressful" (Puff, puff, puff).

What is even funnier is that I have done that with food. A tidal wave could be coming toward the boat; I would have been looking for a snack. Where's the Little Debbies NOW?

Fear of death is a huge stressor; we do the same thing with other stress. What does your programming tell you to do when you are stressed? Do you gain weight, do you smoke more, do you chew your fingernails, or ARE YOU A YELLER?

Identify your stress patterns and the thoughts that cause them, and you can change them. Change your thoughts, change your feelings, change yoiur decisions, change your outcomes.

Making change!

1. **Change your thoughts.**

2. **Change your feelings.**

3. **Change your decisions.**

4. **Change in action will easily follow.**

Change is a process. It starts with a decision or a thought to change: a decision to start running, stop smoking, or lose weight. It also applies to saving money or building better relationships. Understanding how change occurs allows you to make changes based on your goals.

Let's use the example of exercising regularly.

Your Success Experience

Love The Life You Live, Experience Your Success!

Patrick R. Lowe, D.C.

1 Change your thoughts

Research is one of the best ways to do this. Look up articles on your exercise. The internet gives you tons of information. What are the health benefits of exercising 4 times a week? It helps lower blood sugar, preventing type 2 diabetes. It improves muscle mass so you burn more calories when you are not exercising. It decreases stress and burns off the stress hormone, cortisol. Since it decreases your stress, it helps with your relationships. Exercise also lowers your risk of high blood pressure.

2 Change your emotions

Tell yourself, "I like exercising, I like my new body, and I like the results." Spend time with people who exercise regularly. It is well documented that people who have an exercise partner stay on track better than those who do it on their own. Attend an exercise class.

Start looking around at cases where people are suffering from the effects of "not exercising." The stronger the negative emotion toward your old habits and the positive emotion toward your new habits, the stronger it will stick.

Celebrate each of your accomplishments toward your goals. Don't *believe* you can do it, *know* you can do it.

Your Success Experience

Love The Life You Live, Experience Your Success!

Patrick R. Lowe, D.C.

What is the difference between believing and knowing? We believe things that could be true. If I showed you a picture of President Bush and asked, "Do you believe that this man is President Bush?," you could answer, "Yes." You could answer yes because you believe that the man in the picture is George Bush. If I then showed you a video of the same man and he didn't talk like President Bush, you could change your mind. Believing allows a degree of uncertainty.

If you asked me, "Do you believe that your name is Patrick Lowe?" I would answer "NO." I KNOW that my name is Patrick Lowe. There is no degree of uncertainty.

Your goal of change is to associate your new habit strongly enough with positive results that you "KNOW" that it benefits you.

Make decisions based on positive feelings

"Don't go to the grocery store when you're hungry." I learned this during college. When I was hungry, I felt that I needed to buy the cake, the hot dogs, and the hamburgers. Only the hot dogs were on the list. When we make decisions based on "need," we are basing our decisions on fear. Needs are based on our fears of negative consequences. "I need to eat, I need to work, I need to have shelter." Maslow's Hierarchy of Needs shows food, water, and shelter as our basic needs. We put other things in this list because of fear. "I need a new car"; "I need a lot of money." Decisions based on fear are not good decisions. Terrorists know this. Their goal is to cause fear and change your actions. They use fear as a weapon because they know it overrides logic.

More lessons from the dog trainer

We had noticed that our new puppy was skinny and didn't eat very much, so we asked the dog trainer what to do. The trainer advised us to pick up the food! Do not leave it for her all of the time.

She could see the expression of concern on my face. She explained, "When dogs have food down all of the time, they don't feel an urgency to eat. They take a couple of bits of food here and there but never eat much. If you want to encourage her to eat, feed her three times a day and pick up after 20 minutes. She'll get hungrier between times and eat more." (A dog's Success Experience.)

I remembered that a hog farmer told us the same thing 20 years ago. You can never buy just one baby pig; it won't eat and get big. If you add a second pig, they will compete for the food and eat more! (A hog's Success Experience.)

The lesson for us is … Think about what you want. (to be thin, to be healthy) and avoid creating a sense of LACK because of it! The dog felt lack so she ate more; the hogs felt lack because of competition so they ate more. Feelings of deficiency lead to excess consumption, or decisions that don't support our Success Experiences!

We tell ourselves, "This is the only time I get to…", "I only eat _____ times a day", "If I don't do it now, I will not get a chance for 3 hours." None of these thoughts supports our success. They come from a position of deficiency.

We get many small Success Experiences from fulfilling our needs. We act impulsively when we are concerned about not having enough; we overindulge and compete for resources that we think are scarce. These decisions are based on fear. Fear is a negative emotion, and it destroys logic and reverses our progress.

We make good decisions when we see the world as abundant to meet our needs. Be sure to make decisions from an attitude of abundance. To change an action, first change the thoughts and feelings that support it.

3 Change your Decisions

Thoughts + Feelings + Decisions = Actions. What you do is the result of the other changes you have made. If you've done your work on changing your thoughts, feelings and decisions, the change in actions is easy. Your new actions will easily follow.

Your Success Experience

Love The Life You Live, Experience Your Success!

Patrick R. Lowe, D.C.

Your Secret Identity!

How you identify yourself to other people determines how they feel about you. How you identify yourself to you determines how you feel.

We have titles we use, like "I am a smoker, I am slow, I am lazy, I am a stress eater. I am, I am, I am."

Write your own introduction. Speakers are always introduced before they come on stage. "I now give you Patrick Lowe, a Chiropractor, a non-smoker, a dad, a family guy, a writer, a speaker,…"

What would your introduction say to the world? What do you want the world to know about you?

What is your secret identity? How do you present yourself to you? I hear people identify themselves as overweight, as a smoker, as a poor money manager, as a _____ (fill in the blank). They put it on a nametag, on their mirror, and know that that is their identity.

In fact, it is the result of choices. If you don't want that identity anymore, change it. Change your identity statement to a choice statement. If someone asks, "Are you a smoker?" answer "No, I am a non-smoker, I choose to smoke at times." You will be amazed at how empowering this is. It is a whole lot easier to change a choice than to change your identity.

Chapter 4

Eight Most Common Excuses for Being Unsuccessful

And the "Why's" to overcome them

What your friends won't tell you and your enemies don't want you to know

Excuses start out as harmless stories we tell ourselves and others about why we aren't doing something. The more we tell the same excuse the more we believe it. They are ways of justifying our decisions. They become dangerous to our success when we start to defend them with emotion and then believe them.

1. I don't have time

You will never "find" time; every second of every day is used by some activity. These activities seem important at the time, but are they really?

I rarely meet someone who doesn't feel like his or her life is busy. It is true; they are busy, doing something. It is hard to see what they are busy doing because you can't see the results. The adage holds true, "If you want something done, ask a busy person." Busy people are more aware of where their time goes and either tend to waste less time or prioritize their time better than the average person. Perhaps they just know where their time goes and use it better.

Do you know where your time goes?

Let's find out. Write down where you spend your time during the day. Do this every day for two weeks. How much time do you invest traveling to and from work? How much time do you spend at work, doing work? How much time do you invest in building relationships, watching TV, and going to the grocery store?

Now review your list. Assign each a number. Activities that:

1)   Have to be done by me

2) Have to be done by someone

3) Do not have to be done at all

Review your time tracking once more and mark activities that

    A.   prepare me for more Success Experiences

    B.   add value or Success Experiences for others

    C.   do not support more Success Experiences

If it is a Time Waster, mark the TW column and <u>get rid of it</u>.

Your Success Experience

Love The Life You Live, Experience Your Success!

Patrick R. Lowe, D.C.

Time	Activity	1,2,3	A.B.C	T.W.
7-7:15a	Got ready for work	1	A	
7:15-7:30	Ate Breakfast	1	A	
7:30-8:00	Watched TV			X
8-8:30	Drove to Work	1	A	
8:30-8:45	Sorted E-Mails	2	B	
7-8pm	Cut Grass	2	C	
8-9	Exercised	1	A	

You now have your priorities for your time. Now it's time to: Do, Delegate, or Eliminate

- Do the "Activities that have to be done by me"

- Delegate the things that someone else could do (if you can)

- Eliminate the things that don't have to be done at all.

There will always be some dirty dishes. I know, it seems like a radical thought, but it is true. If you don't have any dirty dishes then you probably eat out too much.

I always have some dirty dishes. I tried to blame it on having 4 children, but even when they are with Grandma, there are still dirty dishes, and yes they have to be done, by someone. There will always be grass to mow and floors to vacuum.

In my quest to get higher priority things done, these things sometimes have to wait. I enjoy mowing the grass, once a year. After that it becomes a chore. A chore that everyone in the neighborhood can see when I don't do it. One of my goals was to earn enough money that I could pay a reliable person to take care of my lawn care needs and make me look good. I am very thankful for the man that does it for me; he does a great job and HE enjoys doing it. It is a winning relationship for both of us.

On my time tracking list, mowing the grass is marked as an "Activity that someone has to do." I also blocked it off as an activity that "Doesn't contribute to my Success Experiences or prepare me for them. "

I traded mowing the grass for a similar amount of time with my family, at the office, or promoting the office.

There will always be <u>things</u> to do; how important are those things to reaching your next big Success Experience?

Finally, set your priorities. Are you making decisions to do the most important things each day? Are you making decisions that will prepare you for your next big Success Experience?

What are your five most important goals for this year, the next 6 months, one month, one week? Make a list and keep these things first.

Want to free up time? Unplug your TV.

"You can't do your homework and watch TV at the same time. Watching TV won't help you pass your test." Even though I hated hearing that, my parents were right. One of the largest thieves of our time is the television.

In addition to wasting time, it is very negative and adds negative memories to our memory bank accounts. This is especially true of the news.

Not only is the "News Negative," it reports mostly about the PAST! You can't do ANYTHING to change the past. The few stories they do give about the future are HORRIBLE predictions about things that probably won't even happen!

Last year my good friend, Ryan Bowman, and I went to London. We planned the trip in March and were heading over in August. I don't watch the news. I was sitting at the Louisville airport, ready to catch my flight, and my phone rang. "Doc, did you hear that there is a terrorist threat at Heathrow in London? They just arrested a bunch of people with a plot to blow up planes with liquids." My flight was delayed. Guess what, I heard about it! We went anyway.

> **"You can't do your homework and watch TV at the same time."**
> Mom and Dad

A few months later, we went to

Japan for a business trip. The thing about the news in Japan, even if I watched it, I don't speak Japanese! One night Ryan called his wife and learned that the news in the US had been predicting a huge tidal wave, 100 feet or so, to hit the East Coast of Japan earlier that day. My cell phone doesn't speak Japanese either so... We didn't know about it. I do, however, know that if I see a bunch of people running away from the coast, I will run WITH THEM.

The wave that actually hit the coast was only 16 inches!

2. STRESS!

Who doesn't look at the easy life and say, "I want that, life without stress"?

Did you know that the friction from air slows down an airplane? However, without air the plane can't get any lift and would fall straight to the ground. The same thing that causes stress on the plane, also allows it to fly.

Stress is a necessary part of life. I HATE to hear phrases like controlling stress. What kind of oxymoron is that? How much more stress is created YELLING AT THE KIDS TO STOP CAUSING STRESS! We create stress about controlling stress. Most cases of stress are CAUSED by trying to control or go against something. Stress is a necessary part of life, it teaches us lessons, and if we are smart, we learn from it, do what we need to do, and move on. I hear concerned family members tell a heart patient, "Avoid stress" or "Control your stress!" Just saying that makes EVERYTHING STRESSFUL! I think it is more stressful to think of yourself as a ticking bomb, than it is to get mad in traffic.

There are several different types of stress. They can all be categorized as either good stress or bad stress. It is easy to confuse them. In college, I learned that tests caused me stress. I also learned that, if a test did not cause me stress, I did not study. Pre-test stress was beneficial for me—Good Stress.

> "There has never yet been a man in our history who lived a life of ease whose name is worth remembering."
>
> President Theodore Roosevelt

Bad Stress occurred if I did not study and did poorly on the test. I prevented a lot of bad stress by preparing for the test.

Your Success Experience

Love The Life You Live, Experience Your Success!

Patrick R. Lowe, D.C.

In order to get big muscles you have to stress them by lifting weights or working out. In order to learn and remember new information you have to repeat it over and over. Even your bones require stress. Researchers have discovered that astronauts can lose bone density very rapidly when in space because the lack of gravity/stress. It happens so quickly that after only a few days in space, they were concerned about breaking bones from walking, after returning to earth. In order to battle this, they have installed a system of rubber tubing so astronauts can work out under stress while in space. It is the same with achieving Success Experiences. If your idea of the ultimate Success Experience is a life with NO stress, you are chasing smoke rings.

Life without stress can actually kill you. Medical professionals understand that people's health degenerates rapidly if they retire from productive work. Some researchers estimate that retiring from productive work leads to death in as little as two years.

3. "That is how I was raised."

At age 18, you are old enough and mature enough, by law, to enter into contracts, get credit cards, and vote. At age 21 you are considered responsible enough (by law) to make safe decisions about drinking.

By the time you are 25, you are old enough to start taking responsibility for your own life. If you are over the age of 25 and still blaming your parents for your life, MOVE OUT! Stop blaming your parents for what is going wrong in your life. To continue blaming someone else is to avoid responsibility and avoid changing your life. Get therapy, get a mentor, get successful friends, and get over it!

> **Many authorities believe that *most families* are dysfunctional in some way. That means it is NORMAL to come from a dysfunctional family!**

Many authorities believe that *most families* are dysfunctional in some way. That means it is NORMAL to come from a dysfunctional family! It is no longer an excuse; it doesn't make you more special than the next guy. That is funny! Normally dysfunctional.

Helpless blame, "I can't help it, I grew up that way."

76

Your Success Experience

Love The Life You Live, Experience Your Success!

Patrick R. Lowe, D.C.

"My dad always told me …."

"When we were growing up…"

> **BLAME stands for "Because Losers Always Make Excuses"**

Here is the key: You continued those habits of thinking because you were most comfortable around other people just like you. You grew up like the people around you!

If failure is a family tradition, start a new tradition!

Jesus was eating with a group of people when his family came to take him back home. Can you hear them talking?

"Jesus has lost his mind… he thinks he is a teacher, he is eating with these people. He needs to get back to work to fix Mrs. Jones' table. He wasn't raised like this. We are carpenters, not preachers and missionaries."[9]

Jesus could have said, OK, Mom, let's go home. Instead, he said, "Who are my mother and brothers?" He knew that his journey, his Success Experiences could not be accomplished from home. He said that people who supported his success were his family!

Einstein said, "These problems cannot be solved with the same level of thinking that was present when we created them." As Children, we live at home and learn to think like the people around us. To raise your level of thinking, get outside your comfort zone and spend time with bigger thinkers.

Remember BLAME stands for "Because Losers Always Make Excuses"

Take responsibility for your life and you can change it!

4. I don't play politics!

And YOU SHOULDN'T! We hear "I got passed over for the promotion because of politics." Playing politics means that you are insincerely schmoozing or sucking up to someone in order to get something for yourself. It implies a one-sided relationship. You also shouldn't like someone just for what they can do for you.

> **People who like people are liked by people.**

Many people confuse the idea of Givers Gain for playing politics. Givers Gain is the major premise of the Business

Networking Group, BNI. It says that the more you help someone with their business, the more they will help you.

In all relationships, we want to help people who have helped us and people who we like!

People who like people are liked by people. It is hard to like someone who doesn't like you. The reverse is true as well.

If you want to have more Success Experiences with people,

> **-Find a common interest.**
>
> **-Help them out often.**
>
> **-Get rid of the scorecard.**

- Find common interests. All relationships begin with points of common interest.

- Help them out, often. We tend to reward people who continuously put forth additional effort to help us reach our goals.

- Get rid of the scorecard. Keeping a mental scorecard of things you do for someone else is a dangerous habit for most of your relationships. People who do this have a payback sheet on the other side and, guess what? You each give different value to an event. I think taking you to dinner is worth you cutting my grass! Reply: But you have 10 acres; that would take me 14 hours! Keeping score always leaves someone feeling cheated, usually the scorekeeper.

5. I don't like selling!

That is a common excuse for not being success-full. Selling is an art. You sell your spouse on going out to dinner, you sell your boss on taking a day off, and you sell your kids on going to school every day. Why? Selling is the art of giving information on why something is in someone else's best interest. Salespeople help you make a decision by giving you more information.

When we wanted to buy a new car, the salesman didn't hold a gun up, didn't push us down the stairs; he showed us the car we asked to see, and he gave us honest information and even helped us get financing arranged. Without his assistance we would not have been able to get from where we were (wanting a new car) to where we wanted to be (driving and owning a new car). His Success Experience of selling matched our Success Experience of buying. That is the way it should be!

Your Success Experience

Love The Life You Live, Experience Your Success!

Patrick R. Lowe, D.C.

Robert Kiyosaki writes about this in *Rich Dad, Poor Dad*. He tells the story of a journalist who is interviewing him. She has written a couple of novels, people seem to like them, but they were not picked up by publishers or sold. He explained that she should take some classes in selling. She didn't like selling or salespeople. Her "professional attitude" told her that selling was beneath her. He showed her the front of his book that says, "best-selling author." Robert explained that she was indeed a better writer but he was the better seller. [10]

In consulting with Chiropractors around the country, I have heard this exact same excuse. "I don't think it is professional to do marketing and events to meet people." Some even complain about running an ad in their newspaper. I always ask, "Do you like being broke?"

Everything is sold. Churches sell their message and call it evangelism. Companies sell their products to stores, stores in turn offer them on their shelves to you, and you either see the value and buy it, or you don't.

I have a neighbor who sells die cut parts and machines to companies that make cardboard boxes. These parts make boxes the right size and shape based on their purpose. Without his sales skills, your pizza would come in two flat pieces of cardboard.

Your Success Experience

Love The Life You Live, Experience Your Success!

Patrick R. Lowe, D.C.

The fact is everything that you have in your house got there through the efforts of some salesperson. They sold it to a store chain, where you bought it.

"Build a better mouse trap and the world will beat a path to your door." Author unknown

"if they know about it." Harve Eker [14]

"And they perceive that having mice is a problem!" Pat Lowe

This breaks down to finding a solution to a need, marketing it (telling people about it), and selling it (showing people how it benefits them).

Find a solution to a need… Eating out tonight is a solution to our need to eat.

Market it… "Honey, there is a great new restaurant I heard about."

Sell it… "I know you're tired. Let's go out tonight, it won't be as crowded as on the weekend. You won't have to cook or do the dishes AND the kids can order whatever they want."

People don't like selling for one of three reasons:

- They lack self-confidence and fear being rejected, or

Your Success Experience

- They misunderstand what selling really is, or

- They lack self-confidence and fear rejection because they misunderstand what selling really is.

6. I don't have any money for college…

This statement is usually followed by, "and I don't want to take out student loans." The only thing worse than having student loans … is *not* having student loans and the increased income potential that they bring. It made sense to me to invest $20,000 in my student loans so I could earn an additional $10,000-$20,000 a year for the next 30 years. I have never had a banker offer me that kind of return.

7. Life is not fair!

Thank Goodness! I was talking with Alex today, and he said, "It's not fair!" As a parent, I have heard that a lot. When you are nine and your brother is seven, many things seem unfair. In the past, I have just commented, "Life is not fair, we all get used to it." Tonight was different. Our conversation started like always. "It's not fair; he got one more _____ than I did." I replied, "Life is not fair, thank goodness." You could have knocked him over with a feather. "What?" he said.

Love The Life You Live, Experience Your Success!

Patrick R. Lowe, D.C.

"Life is not fair, thank goodness. If everything was always fair, you could never win a race. Everyone would finish at the same time. That would be fair, right?"

"In a fair world, everyone who put in the same amount of time and energy training would finish at the same time."

"I guess so," he replied.

"Everyone would get a gold medal; it wouldn't be very encouraging, would it?"

"I guess not." "I'm glad it's not fair, too, I like to win."

"It's not just about winning. Sometimes things are unfair and they go against you. When you realize it, you can wait for the time when it is unfair in your favor."

"OK, can I play computer now?"

He lost interest at that point. Saying it out loud made it sink in for me. It isn't really that life isn't fair; it is our limited perception of our needs that makes it seem unfair. Hurricanes that destroyed the towns along the Gulf Coast did not pick which house to destroy. They destroyed them all. Tornadoes that hit the Midwest towns have the same chance of hitting a church as they do hitting a barn or outhouse. The Bible says,

"He maketh his sun to rise on the evil and on the good, and sendeth rain on the just and on the unjust." Mathew 5:45

People are sometimes unfair. Life is not. If you are dealing with unfair people, change the people you deal with. If life seems unfair, change you.

8. I lack self-discipline!

I want to lose weight but I lack the self-discipline to do so. Now I am 50 pounds overweight. I lack the self-discipline to quit smoking. I lack the self-discipline to save money.

How much self-discipline does it take to go to the store, stock up on additional food, prepare additional food, and eat tons of food to keep your weight up? It takes a lot! It is on autopilot.

How much self-discipline is required to "never leave home" without an adequate supply of cigarettes and a lighter or matches? It requires a lot. This too is on autopilot.

How much self-discipline is required not get in your car, drive to a store, find a parking space, walk into the store, try on the clothes, wait in line, pay the cashier, walk back to your car, drive home, and put it away? This requires a lot of effort and a lot of self-discipline.

Your Success Experience

Love The Life You Live, Experience Your Success!

Patrick R. Lowe, D.C.

Lack of self-discipline is not the problem. Changing behaviors (actions) without changing the thoughts and feelings behind them doesn't work. Working the equation in the wrong order, like pushing a rope.

Changing the thoughts and feelings first makes changing your behaviors easy. It is like pulling a rope.

Victimology 101

Some people find their Success Experience indirectly from being a victim! It is always someone else's fault. If they buy a losing lottery ticket, they blame the cashier. A victim believes that everyone is trying to take advantage of him, cheat him, or otherwise do him harm. Victims have very low self-esteem, and that is very hard to overcome.

> "Only by taking responsibility for your life can you change it."
>
> Dr. Chuck Gibson

Some people fail out of school because bookwork is difficult for them. School is not for everyone. Different people have different

86

strengths. However, if your blame your failure on, "the teachers not liking you," you are a victim.

If you lose numerous jobs because the boss does not like you, you are a victim.

If you are "ripped off" by every garage you ever take your car to, or always get an "idiot" to work with you at the hospital, you are a victim.

If you repetitively choose mates who drink too much, but you meet all of your mates in bars.....HMMM.

"Only by taking responsibility for your life can you change it." Dr. Chuck Gibson

DO NOT BE A VICTIM! Read to the end of this book and I will show you how to program you brain for success.

If you are comfortable in your role as a victim, please put this book down right now and tell your friends what great colors are on the cover!

*For those of you who read on, it is not that I love the colors on the cover; these people would later blame me for their lack of success if they read the whole book.

The 5 Why's to overcome Excuses

"Some people change jobs, mates, and friends but never think of changing themselves." John Maxwell [8]

Most parents remember the questions of a 3-year-old trying to understand his world. They ask "Why?" three thousand times a day.

Toyota, the number one car manufacturer, uses a technique to get to the root of a problem by asking "Why?" five times. Each answer leads to another, which leads to another and finally another. [16]

> "Some people change jobs, mates, and friends but never think of changing themselves."
>
> John Maxwell

In psychology, there is an entire system of therapy based on the "Why" question.

Input any problem...

"I was late to work." Why?

"Well, traffic was slow and I hit every stop light." Why?

"I hit rush hour traffic." Why?

Your Success Experience

Love The Life You Live, Experience Your Success!

Patrick R. Lowe, D.C.

"I left the house late." Why?

"I overslept." Why?

"I stayed up too late watching a movie."

In reality, it was not the traffic, rush hour, or anything else that was outside of your control that made you late. It was your decision to stay up late and watch a movie.

At Toyota the five Why's get to other systems issues. Elizabeth Haas Edersheim explains: Toyota notices oil on the floor under a machine. Why? It has a leaky gasket. Why is the gasket leaky? It is a less expensive gasket. Why are we using inexpensive gaskets? The buying department ordered inexpensive gaskets. Why? We reward them for lowering costs. The solution is to change the way that we compensate the buyers for their buying decisions. This approach gets to the root of the problem instead of just covering it up. [16]

Why should we use it? To beat the blame game, it cuts through some of the "stuff" that we tell ourselves and shows us who is most responsible for events in our lives. US!

If you can take responsibility for what you have control over, you can change it in a positive way.

Identify which part of the problem you can influence or change. Ask yourself, "With what I know now, would I make the same decision again?"

If you answered "YES," nothing will change and you are destined to relive the same situation and have very similar results.

If you answered "NO," you have learned a lesson and can have better results next time.

It's the LAW!

Gratitude

One of most overlooked laws is the law of gratitude. We are accustomed to a courtesy "Thank you for shopping at _____," or "Thanks for the flowers." That is not true gratitude. True gratitude goes a lot deeper. People recognize true gratitude and respond to it.

The more you appreciate what you have and where you are, the more opportunities you will find to have more and be somewhere else.

True gratitude falls under recognition, appreciation, and approval. You recognize what someone has done or given to you.

Appreciate the gift and approve of the gift. The most valuable gift you can get is someone's time. Time is truly limited for everyone. You cannot make more.

It makes people feel good and want to help you again.

Most people feel undervalued and insignificant. True gratitude adds value to their lives.

"More than prayer changing things for you, prayer often changes you for things." Anonymous

Gratitude is the same way. Not only does it make the other person feel good and add value to them, it adds value to you. The attitude of gratitude adds more positive memories to your memory bank.

How do we show gratitude? There are expected times, like after someone does something for you directly. Call them just to say thank you, not "thank you but..." or "thank you by the way...." Just "Thank You."

A thank you card after receiving a gift, a wedding shower, or an invitation to a party are all customary times to say thank you; they are appreciated and expected.

Unexpected gratitude is even better. It is the difference between sending flowers for a holiday and sending a "just because you are you" bouquet. Unexpected gratitude stands out and adds even more value.

As much as gratitude changes things for you, it changes you for things and increases your Success Experiences.

Thank you for being YOU!

Chapter 5

Your Vision

Discover your vision

"Your young men shall have visions and your old men shall dream dreams." Acts 2:17

> **A vision is a dream with a plan and a possibility for the future.**

I hear and read a lot about dreams. Everyone has dreams. One of the most famous statements about this is from Dr. Martin Luther King, the great civil rights leader, when he said, and "I have a dream." It was a very important dream.

Dr. King actually had a vision of the future. What is the difference between a dream and a vision?

Dreams occur in our minds when we sleep or sometimes when we are awake. Dreams can include all kinds of things from unicorns to pink elephants; they do not point us in any direction. Most importantly, dreams do not specify time; they can be in the past, the future, or the present.

A vision, on the other hand, refers only to the future. You probably don't know all of the details of HOW your vision will come true. You probably do not know when your vision will be fulfilled. A vision has to be for the future.

A vision is a dream with a plan and a possibility for the future.

If you do not know where you are, where you're going does not matter.

Analyzing how you think, seeing where you are now is a HUGE step toward enjoying the life of your dreams. The next step is to develop a personal growth plan and to prepare for future Success Experience opportunities. People change when it "looks good enough or hurts bad enough." Unfortunately, it is easiest to let our autopilot run our lives until it hurts bad enough to change. Then, we put all of our energy into taking away the hurt. You will notice, I did not say getting well, I said taking away the hurt.

The goal with this type of response is to get back to where you started in a comfortable place without pain, where you can start your autopilot up until it hurts again. It doesn't help you grow.

Making my visions become Success Experiences!

Vision Casting

What is your vision of your goal, how will you feel when you get this Success Experience? Who will be with you and what will they say or feel? What will the weather be like?

My seven- and nine-year-old sons have a gift for planning an event, a day, or a Success Experience. While some of their ideas don't come to fruition, they find the most fun out of planning it, thinking about it, dreaming about the details. It is easy for them to dream. "Dad, here is my sketch of the clubhouse." The presentation was coming from my seven-year-old son, Spencer. He has been adding details to his plan every day and cannot wait for me to get home so he can tell me all about it.

"What is this?," I asked.

"That's the secret tunnel so we can get from our basement to our clubhouse without the girls seeing us."

Your Success Experience

Love The Life You Live, Experience Your Success!

Patrick R. Lowe, D.C.

The game between the boys and the girls had really heated up when the girls in our neighborhood offered to put "make-up" on the boys if they caught them. The boys knew that they would have to defend themselves. Planning began immediately. A secret tunnel to a not-so-secret "Boys ONLY" clubhouse seemed the perfect solution.

Not only would they need a secret tunnel, they would need security guards. "The guards will have water balloons to scare away the girls if they come around," said Alex. "Here is the list of all of the club members."

"And I made up a list of who to invite to the clubhouse party. Mom helped me." Spencer was a great writer. For spelling, he counted on Mom. His list had to be right, the details are very important.

"The guards will also have smoke bombs, so the girls don't see us run away," laughed Alex.

The details of their clubhouse included everything from the furniture they wanted to the windows, curtains, and rug they planned to use to cover up the secret trap door in the floor.

Their vision was perfect. The details were complete.

Your Success Experience

Love The Life You Live, Experience Your Success!

Patrick R. Lowe, D.C.

I loved every minute of their presentation. You could feel their excitement about their plans, not just an excitement, a passion.

That is a vision. They knew exactly what they wanted, who they wanted to build it, and what the finished product was going to look like. Most of all, they knew how it was going to feel when they sat in the clubhouse and plotted their next coup to catch the girls.

Many visions do not come true because we are fearful of what other people think. "They might think I am crazy." You would be in good company. Concerned, family and friends admitted Mr. Marconi into an insane asylum for his vision. He believed that he could send sound through the air, over long distances, in invisible waves. He could then catch these waves and convert them back into sounds. He did not know exactly how he was going to do it. Sound crazy? He made his idea work and invented the radio!

Speaker, author, and motivator Les Brown cast his vision time after time, year after year, to everyone he met. "I am going to go on the Robert Shuller Show…" the most popular show. People would reply, "When?" "I don't know yet, do you know him?" Guess who was a guest on Robert Shuller's show? That is right, Les Brown. [12]

Six degrees from vision to Success Experience

A game called 6 degrees of separation from Kevin Bacon was very popular few years ago. This theory holds that fewer than 6 people separate anyone on the planet from anyone else. For example, Sally (your co-worker) dated Steve, who worked with Amy, whose sister works for a talent agent, who works for Sylvester Stallone, who was in a movie with Kevin Bacon.

Our boys are now within 4 degrees of finding someone to build their clubhouse.

Cast your vision before enough people, long enough, and the odds are that you will find someone who shares part or all of your vision with you. People like helping other people fulfill their vision. A Success Experience for both of you!

"Where there is no vision, the people perish!" Proverbs 29:18

It's the LAW!

Law of Equal Exchange

"No relationship will endure unless both parties benefit in equal measure." Dr. Chuck Gibson

Any time that a relationship is out of balance for an extended period, it will fail.

The easiest example of this is with money. Have you ever lost a friend over money? John owes you 20 bucks from a loan last week. You ask him for it once or twice and he never seems to have it on him. It will not take long for one of you to start to resent the other. You may even forget about it, but he knows he owes you. He starts coming around less and the relationship becomes strained.

The same holds true for other things as well. Say you have a friend who eats at your house all of the time. He offers to mow your grass for you to pay you back. This law says that you should let him. You are causing imbalance in the relationship by refusing his offer.

Chapter 6

Life is a TEAM SPORT!

In the United States, our school system rewards individual accomplishments, molding children into well-rounded individuals and measuring individual progress through tests and assignments. It is a competitive system, where we compete with grades, ACT and SAT scores. Students receive scholarships and entrance into the next level of education, college, or graduate school for *individual* test scores. We train people to be independent, so they can do it themselves, on their own. We even talk about the "Self-Made Man." I am a firm believer in the value of a good education. At some point, we need to teach our kids how to build their team.

We live in an information age. We have access to more information now than at any other time in history. Through the internet, you can check your e-mail, learn what the weather is like in Tokyo, and research new cars. We are in a knowledge era. In technology, information doubles and changes every 90 days. What was true yesterday may not be true today. Think of our laws. How quickly can they change?

100

Your Success Experience

Love The Life You Live, Experience Your Success!

Patrick R. Lowe, D.C.

With all of that information to learn and process, teamwork is more important now than ever before. Even if you were a super genius and able to remember and process it all, who has the time? The tax code alone is so complicated that it boggles the minds of those who created it. Cars are more complicated than in the past and personally, I don't like working on them. My team is made up of a tax person, an accountant, a carpenter, a mechanic, a proofreader, and even a cleaning person (I don't like to do that either). I respect each of them for their accomplishments and their skills.

Before I learned this, I would spend several hours working on a project that was not one of my strengths. I would end up spending much more time and money than if I had hired someone do it right the first time. Even worse, I would put off doing something that I did not like doing. I would agonize over it for days or weeks, instead of just getting the job done.

Life is a team sport. All team sports require referees, players, and coaches.

Find your referees

Any team that is playing any sport needs officials or referees. Referees are people who are impartial and "call it like they see it." They keep the game moving and prevent many of the fights that occur in a sandlot game. No one likes the criticism of having a call go against him or her.

John Maxwell calls them truth tellers. These are among the most important people on your team. Without them, the game does not even start.

Referees tell you the truth about your actions, strengths, and non-strengths. Remember the truth often is painful for a short period, but benefits you in the end.

One truth teller comes to mind for me. Her name is Betty. She is a patient and a good friend. After being under care at the office for about 6 months, we had developed a friendship. She said she wanted to talk with me in private.

"Doc, look me in the eye and know that I am only telling you this because I love you. The Bible says speak the truth in love and that is what I am doing for you. When I first started with you, you gave me a great presentation about what my problems were. I am sure it was great, but I couldn't understand you. You mumble, and I think this is holding you back. I just wanted you to know. I think you are a terrific doctor and you have helped me a lot."

That was all that she said to me. My first response was to be defensive. Maybe it is *her* hearing. Later that day I decided that she was right. I picked up the yellow pages and called a vocal instructor. I started lessons to correct my challenges with clear communication.

This alone opened up a world of opportunities that I would not have had otherwise. I am now traveling, speaking to large groups of people, and consulting with other doctors and businesses.

None of this would have been possible if it were not for my friend, the referee and truth teller. Guess who I turned to for feedback on this book? I called my friend, Betty Hundley.

Referees prevent a lot of embarrassment. Many reality television shows have a "worst of" episode where they run their worst auditions. This is one of their most popular episodes, but who really wants to be on it?

Identify who your referees are and thank them for their contribution to your Success Experiences.

Why do I need coaches and mentors?

"I know the rules; I can do it on my own."

There are three levels of knowing.

Love The Life You Live, Experience Your Success!

Patrick R. Lowe, D.C.

1. Knowing **what** you don't know. You can go research it and enlist specific people to help you.

2. Knowing **that** you don't know. You can spend a lot of time trying to learn what you do not know about it and then trying to learn it. You can try to read up on the subject but may miss a lot in the interpretation of the information.

3. **Not knowing** that you don't know or what you do not know. This is where most people get stuck. It is nearly impossible to overcome on your own. You do not know that you are deficient in that area.

Coaches and mentors bring years of experience and knowledge; they guide you through all three of the levels and help you interpret the information correctly. Their interest is your best interest.

Identify your coaches and mentors

Tiger Woods is the highest paid, most successful golfer in history. He has a golf coach that works with him on a daily basis. Tiger's mentors included his dad, along with other professional golfers. Now he is a mentor.

Your Success Experience

Love The Life You Live, Experience Your Success!

Patrick R. Lowe, D.C.

Coaches and mentors help you to develop in the area of their specialty. In life, the only difference between a coach and a mentor is that a coach is a paid professional in the field they are helping you with. Most mentors don't wear a badge that says, "MENTOR," they just do it. They take an interest in you and your success.

I have had several coaches and several mentors in my life. Many of my coaches go beyond just coaching and mentor in other areas as well.

I utilize a Chiropractic office coach, Voice Coach, Martial Arts Coach, and we have had a Dance Coach.

Finding mentors

Choose mentors who have Success Experiences, talents, or skills that you want or need to acquire. Based on where you are and where you want to go, who can help you get there? Do you have a relationship with a person who has experience in this area?

There are two categories of mentors, Personal Mentors and Group Mentors.

<u>Personal Mentors</u> talk with you in a small group or individually. Keep in mind the law of equal exchange. How can you add value to the potential mentor? Focus on giving and you will surely receive in return. It is about forming a winning relationship for both of you.

<u>Group Mentors</u> work with a large group at once or "on demand." Do not ignore this type of mentor. They have to organize their thoughts and programs into a book, like this one. They want to help anyone who will put in the effort. My goal with this book is to help you have more Success Experiences.

I have had several coaches and mentors in my life. Some I have worked for, some I have hired, and some have volunteered. Others, I pay to work with or for, in order to learn from them. A coach or mentor has facilitated every step of my Success Experience. They each have experience in different fields, but most of all they each have been patient with my development. They are positive people who take a genuine interest in you, not for what you can do for them, but what they can do for you. They are patient and encouraging, and they do not mind repeating the same lesson, over and over and over again, until you get it. Most of all, they have faith in you! They know that you WILL get it, so they do not give up.

Short list of my mentors:

My parents Dr. Randy Lowe, Sandy Lowe; Dr. Darrell Fore, Dr. Chuck Gibson, Dr. Jay Morgan, Grand Master Jung Oh Hwang, G.W. Rodgers, Dr. Mike Shell, Dr. Mark Beaty, Drs. Ryan and Christine Bowman, Dr. Dana O'Neal, George Thompson, Mr. Ogawa, Mr. Dan Cassin, Mary Heady—the list is almost endless.

What is your TF (Teach-ability Factor)?

Mentors and coaches are all around if you are ready to learn. Do you want to learn? Are you truly teachable? People are willing to help you if you are willing to learn. The old adage, "When the pupil is ready, the teacher will be there" holds true. Everyone I meet can teach me something. Books are among the best gifts I have ever received.

I have had opportunities to mentor other Chiropractors. One doctor worked for me. He seemed to lack self-confidence and had challenges in his personal and professional relationships. I frequently loaned him books to help him grow and learn.

When I would ask how he was progressing with a book, he would say, "I'm almost done, Doc." I suspected that he was not reading the books as he said.

At our staff Christmas party, I gave him a cash bonus and two books. I had meticulously selected both books to help him with his challenges. I really wanted him to have more Success Experiences, financial Success Experiences and personal Success Experiences.

> **The biggest key to learning is being teachable!**

Toward the back of one of the books, I taped a ONE HUNDRED dollar bill. I made sure it was nice and flat so he would not find it by accident. He would have a great bonus for reading the book.

He has since moved on to another job, in another city. He has never found that $100 bill. I suspect that he sold the book for $4 to a used bookstore when he moved.

His teach-ability factor was very low.

108

Your Success Experience

Love The Life You Live, Experience Your Success!

Patrick R. Lowe, D.C.

Here are some of the attributes of teachable people I have known. They

- actively seek feedback on their performance,

- welcome constructive criticism,

- put information into action quickly,

- are slow to criticize others,

- are not afraid to make mistakes,

- like trying new things,

- ask questions,

- read books to learn new ideas and skills,

- listen to motivational tapes and CD's,

- identify their truth tellers and ask for feedback.

The biggest key to learning is being teachable!

What player positions to fill?

Speaker and business consultant George Thompson says, "Third basemen don't go to the all-star game to play first base. They go and play third base, a first baseman plays first base, the same with the pitcher, catcher and shortstop. Play *your* position and play it well. Let the rest of the team play *their* positions and then you have a winning all-star team."

> **"Third basemen don't go to the all-star game to play first base."**
>
> George Thompson

What position best suits you? What are your strengths, what do you like to do? What do you not like to do? Are you quiet and shy or are you talkative and outgoing?

Take some time to get to know yourself. Myers-Briggs and other personality tests can be performed online and give you some personal insight. You can also buy copies of these tests at bookstores.

When you know your strengths, you can build on them and recruit assistance with your non-strengths.

Ask trusted friends and family to help you identify your strengths and non-strengths. We all need truth tellers in our lives. Do not be offended by their answers.

> "The best way to get everything you want out of life is to help enough other people get what they want out of life."
>
> Zig Ziglar

Once you know what position best suits you, you can build the rest of your team. The good news is you do not have to limit it to nine players.

My team for this book includes five content editors, two spelling and grammar editors, a layout editor, a graphics person, several idea consultants, a printer, and a publisher. All of that is for one book.

Getting help from other people

"It is one of the most beautiful compensations in life.... we can never help another without helping ourselves." Ralph Waldo Emerson

As a rule, people love helping other people. Several attributes will make you more attractive to receiving help.

> "... we can never help another without helping ourselves."
>
> Ralph Waldo Emerson

Dr. Ivan Misner started a very popular business-networking group called Business Networking International. In their meetings, everyone stands up and talks about their business. During the next week, members search for opportunities to help other members get more business. Their mantra is "Givers Gain." The more you help other people in the group, the more they will work to help you.

Motivational speaker and writer Zig Ziglar says, "The best way to get everything you want out of life is to help enough other people get everything they want out of life." [7]

Your Success Experience

Love The Life You Live, Experience Your Success!

Patrick R. Lowe, D.C.

People like to help people they like.

Think for a minute about the people who you just cannot wait to see. Every time you see them, they show that they cannot wait to see you either. The people I can't wait to see... Smile when they see me. They can't wait to talk to me. They are happy and enthusiastic. To sum it up, they are fun.

> **A true friend is happy for your successes and celebrates with you.**

Everyone wants to have fun! The best way to draw a crowd is to have fun. Psychiatrist Cliff Kuhn calls it "The Fun Factor." [17] The more we have fun in what we are doing, the more people want to be involved.

People like positive people and they like encouragement. Real genuine interest in what interests them. A true friend is happy for your successes and celebrates with you.

Have you heard the saying, "A friend in need is a friend indeed"? That is partly true. When I talk to my kids, I say, "A friend in success, you'll find much less." Be the friend in success.

Your Success Experience

Love The Life You Live, Experience Your Success!

Patrick R. Lowe, D.C.

I hear people complaining, "Once he got money, he didn't want to hang around me anymore." I ask, "Were you happy for him?" "Of course I was. Now he has all that money and doesn't share any of it."

A true friend would not ask or expect him to! They would be happy for his success. Research on lottery winners shows that many of them are broke within 5 years, in part because of expectations of friends and family to give them money. They either lose their money or lose their friends.

If you really want people to like you and help you, add value to their lives. Celebrate their successes with them.

We all CRAVE true admiration, positive attention, affirmation. The more you become the lifter, them more you will be lifted up. We often have the misconception that leaders are at the front of the line and everyone else follows.

I love to tell the story of the 10 men stranded in Alaska. They had decided to vacation in Alaska. Each would get a team of sled dogs and they would take a "manly" vacation.

Your Success Experience

Love The Life You Live, Experience Your Success!

Patrick R. Lowe, D.C.

They did not realize that you have to tie your dogs up at night, away from the sleds, so their dogs ran off, leaving 10 men and one sled. After some careful discussion, they decided that nine of them would pull the sled and one would ride. Each man insisted that he should be the leader, the one in front, the alpha male. The biggest, loudest, strongest man insisted that he lead the team, up front. The rest of the men took their places behind him. If you have ever seen a pack of sled dogs, you know that the one who actually leads the pack is the man in the back with the whip! He is the true encourager.

Truett Cathy, the founder of the Chick-fil-A restaurant chain, asks, "How do you know when someone needs encouragement? When they are breathing." [5]

> **"How do you know when someone needs encouragement? When they are breathing."**
>
> Truett Cathy

Leadership is more about encouraging than being the first to pull. There will never be an over-abundance of encouragement.

Your Success Experience

Love The Life You Live, Experience Your Success!

Patrick R. Lowe, D.C.

Everyone loves an Encourager. They use the principles of recognition, appreciation, and approval.

Encouragers are never short of friends or people who will return the favor. If you want people to be on your team and help you out, be on their team and help them out.

> **Encouragers are never short of friends or people who will return the favor.**

It's the LAW!

Law of Attraction

We attract into our lives the things we think about most. This goes hand in hand with the Law of Conscious Awareness. Once you start thinking about a thing, you notice opportunities that allow you to obtain it.

I started talking to my kids about this law.

Alexander started thinking about it and said, "I want a force-activated light saber." "You already have 3 light sabers and that one is a lot more expensive," I replied.

He returned a few minutes later to show me a picture of his force-activated light saber taped to his wall.

"I am going to use the law of attraction to get it," he quipped.

"OK," I said, slightly skeptical.

Three weeks later, he had a force-activated light saber.

He had found a way to get what he had on his mind.

Many opportunities are overlooked when we are not looking for them. The Law of Attraction helps us spot the opportunities to make vision become reality. It also prompts us to prepare for potential opportunities.

Amazingly, it happens all of the time. What you think about tends to come true. It allows us to prepare for opportunities and to see them when they arrive.

The Law of Attraction works for negative thoughts as well. Your subconscious mind works to prove you right. Henry Ford said, "Whether you think you can or cannot, you are right." Be sure to focus and think about what you want instead of what you do not want.

Chapter 7

Kaizen

Kaizen is the Japanese word meaning small daily improvements. This technique prevents the large gaps between your big Success Experiences. Kaizen prepares us for Success Experiences that we never would have even thought of before.

1. Reading

"You are today what you'll be five years from now, except for the people you meet and the books you read." Charlie Tremendous Jones [18]

Read books and magazines that interest you and help you grow. *People* magazine, the local newspaper, and the *National Inquirer* are entertaining but provide little useful information to help you grow.

Your Success Experience

Love The Life You Live, Experience Your Success!

Patrick R. Lowe, D.C.

President Harry S. Truman said, "Not all readers are leaders but all leaders must be readers."

I like reading books on leadership, self-improvement, psychology, health, and business. You may like art, music, and history. If one of your ideal Success Experiences is to do mission work or go on an archeological dig, then read about those things.

> **"Not all readers are leaders but all leaders must be readers."**
>
> President Harry S. Truman

Pat Williams, the Sr. Vice President of the Orlando Magic, gave these statistics at a lecture:

"The average man, upon graduating from high school will never read another book."

"Only 5% of people will ever set foot in a book store."

"If you read 5 books on any one subject you will be a world leading authority on that subject." [19]

I challenge all of my staff to read a minimum of one book a month on a subject that interests them. Reading is one of the best investments you can make in your future. It allows you to be mentored from hundreds of miles away.

"Man's mind, once stretched by a new idea, never regains its original dimensions." Oliver Wendell Holmes, Sr. [20]

2. Affirmations

I have been talking with people and I ask them if they do affirmations. Many of them say, "No." The fact is that they do; we do affirmations all day every day we are alive. Our affirmations are both verbal and nonverbal in nature. An affirmation is any statement that reinforces an idea. An affirmation is any word, thought, or action that supports another word, thought, or action. It can be positive or negative.

Marketing people tell us that it takes over 26 exposures of an advertisement for us to remember the name of a new product—26. It takes more exposures than that to change a behavior.

The use of positive affirmations day after day, week after week, year after year will reprogram your mind in whatever way you want it to.

Verbal affirmations

"Out of the abundance of the heart the mouth speaketh."Mathew 12:34 Our words reflect our feelings.

To change the outcomes, change your feelings. Verbal affirmations are the best way to reprogram your thoughts, which in turn change your feelings.

Most experts on affirmations recommend that you write your own affirmations.

Write your own affirmations,

with a deadline,

based on what you want,

as if they have already occurred,

with a positive emotion added.

Example:

> Today is July 31, 2007
>
> My working out is a lot of fun and showing great progress, I am under 160 now and I look terrific. I am very excited!

Read your affirmations aloud twice a day.

Nonverbal affirmations

Body posture and body language are among the hardest to see, yet they are most important affirmations we give ourselves. We intuitively read other people's body language. It tells us a lot about what they are NOT saying. Someone walks in the room, looking at the floor, not making eye contact. He doesn't talk to anyone, just takes his seat. You assume that he is either really shy or depressed.

A lady walks in the room with a big smile on her face, talking to people, making eye contact, and walking to her seat quickly. She appears confident.

We typically don't pay much attention to our own body language and posture, but others do. Our thoughts and feelings send messages to muscles in our bodies. Then our

123

bodies send messages back to our brains telling us how we are feeling.

Someone who is stressed or depressed shows a grimace on his face. They look at the floor and see the cracks, which only increases their feelings of depression.

Someone who is relaxed and happy smiles, makes eye contact, and looks up to notice the sky is clear and the sun is shining!

When we slump, walk slowly, and frown, we are telling ourselves that we feel bad. When we walk briskly, smile, and look up, we are telling ourselves, and the world, that we are happy, successful people. Whatever your posture is telling you, your brain believes.

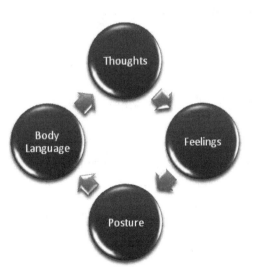

Try this: Look down at the floor for ½ a day and see how it makes you feel.

Look up at the sky for ½ a day and see how that makes you feel.

People have known

Your Success Experience

Love The Life You Live, Experience Your Success!

Patrick R. Lowe, D.C.

---

that for centuries, and we talk about it when we say things like "Digging a hole to hell" versus "going up to heaven." When you get in trouble and keep talking anyway, we say you are "digging yourself deeper." When someone gives you a compliment, you are "uplifted."

If posture and body language tell other people how we feel, our posture and body language scream at us.

To improve your Success Experiences, improve your posture.

What is good posture? Look at yourself in a picture or a mirror. From the side, your ear should be straight over your shoulder and your shoulder straight over your hips. From the front, your shoulders should be level, your ears level, and your hips level.

Body language.

If you're happy, tell your face and smile. If you're not happy and want to be, tell your face and smile—I mean really smile.

In his book *The Fun Factor,* Psychiatrist Cliff Kuhn prescribes facial exercises to strengthen your smile muscles. [17]

Teaching ourselves the "bad" life!

How we learn and teach ourselves.

I never took this class in school; I wish it had been offered. I learned a lot of it through my psychology classes in my senior year of college. The more senses involved with your studying, the easier it will stick with you. The rule is read it, write it, say it, hear it, associate it, and know it. To read it, you use your eyes, which send information to one part of your brain for processing. Writing or taking notes goes to another part. Saying it does two things: One, it engages the processing part of your brain that makes sounds, and, two, you hear it. You can't talk without hearing yourself.

Associate it: We retain information most easily when we put it together with something we already know. If you know the name of a street is Alexander Street and you want to remember it, associate it with an image of your friend Alexander.

The easiest way to do all of this quickly is through study groups. Each member of the group reads it before they meet. One person quizzes others, and then they switch roles. Take notes on what you missed. Associations often take care of themselves in the conversations.

126

Now you know it. A few repetitions and it will stick.

We unknowingly learn negative experiences by creating a story and telling it over and over again. When we tell the story, our friends naturally ask us about the details of it (quiz us). We retell the story later to someone else, which reinforces the negative experience even more. When we retell it we relive it, say it, hear it, and sometimes even write it down. All of this teaches us how bad our lives are—another case of negative affirmations.

Turning our negative affirmations positive

Our words express how we feel. We say things not only to other people but also to ourselves. The things we say to ourselves are the most dangerous. We tell ourselves things like "I am not as successful as I want to be," "I am not wealthy," and "I am not as thin as I want to be."

Never lie to yourself; you will always get caught. Untrue affirmations can be detrimental.

Write your affirmations in a positive light and remember your echo machine. "I am becoming more successful every day." "I am practicing Kaizen and I am excited about my future."

Your Success Experience

Love The Life You Live, Experience Your Success!

Patrick R. Lowe, D.C.

We also ask ourselves negative questions. Did you reach your goal? The answer to the problem lies in one word… "Yet."

"Yet" allows your mind to see the possibility of what you want. It opens up your mind to the idea that you will accomplish your goal.

I am not as successful as I want to be YET. I am not rich YET, I am not as thin as I want to be YET, and I have not reached my goal YET. Can you see how a little change in words changes the feelings?

Visualization

Research on visualization shows that real and imagined experiences have nearly the same effect on performance.

Think of your most memorable Success Experience. Can you remember the praise of your friends and the feeling of pride that came with your success? What smells were around you? How did it feel?

Your memories of the past help you visualize your future. Psychologists tell us that our memories of smells are the most potent memories. My grandfather smoked a pipe. Thirty

128

years later, the smell of "Captain Black" pipe tobacco takes me right back. I start recalling the great memories of our times together, things we did, the house he lived in, even his car.

It is easy for me to put the smell of Captain Black tobacco into my visualizations. It gives my visualizations a warm fuzzy feeling, adds a strong positive emotion, and helps me realize my visions. Associating your strong emotional memories with your vision of the future helps make it come true. With enough repetition, your brain will assume that your Success Experience has already occurred and make it easier to accomplish.

3. Your own advertisements

Selling you on you!

Advertisers tell us that it takes 26 exposures for us to learn and remember the name of a new product. They use varied techniques to get the information into our brains. They do not stop advertising on exposure number 27. The idea in advertising is to keep the name in front of the customer at all times. The same is true for your desired Success Experiences;

you have to keep them in front of you at all times. If you don't, other things will begin to dominate your thoughts.

I recently attended a meeting of Advertising Agencies. The two most successful advertising techniques are "User-Generated Content" and "The Experience."

Generate your content

User-generated content is when people are able to affect the actions or outcomes of an advertisement. It is the ability to personalize it in some way. Pepsi is running an online campaign where patrons design their own Pepsi can.

Career Builders put out Monkey Mail. You could send an e-mail with a talking monkey in it to your friends. You could personalize what it looked like, the background, and even its accent.

Do the same for yourself by making up some advertising pages for your long-term Success Experiences. Take magazines with pictures of what you want and make a collage of different pictures of the experiences you want. It may be a new car. For more impact, get a picture of yourself in that new car. Look at it 3 times a day.

Create the experience

The army has several challenges in recruiting right now: We are currently at war, the army is the least glamorous of the armed forces, and media coverage has been less than favorable. One advertising agency has designed a program to help the army with their recruiting.

The army sets up a 23,000-square-foot tent. A potential recruit gets to be the gunner on a simulation of going into battle. They meet their team. They begin their mission, the adrenaline begins to pump, as the soldiers yell orders and warnings. They get a score for their performance. At the end of the adventure, the recruit is excited. They leave with an ID badge and a memory to last a lifetime. Recruiters say that it is the most effective tool they have had. It leaves little to the imagination.

Young people stand in line for hours to have the experience and many of them sign up.

Apply that learning technique to your goals and your brain will sign up too. If you want a new car, go look at them, sit in one. How does it smell, how do your hands feel on the steering wheel? Get your picture taken in the car and add it to your self-advertisement board.

4. Improving your memory for good

The best way to make sure you have mostly Success Experiences in your memory bank is to keep a daily list of successes and blessing. What good things happened today? List at least two things each day. At the end of the week review it and craft a story of your week using only these positive events.

Sunday: Went to church. We cooked out and had a great conversation. Then we went to the pool for an hour. It was a great day!

Monday: Went home for lunch, Caleb was so funny. He was telling jokes and cracking himself up! Wrote 3 more pages of the book.

Tuesday: Got a call from my good friend, his 2-year-old daughter wanted to talk to me. It just made my day! Wrestled with the boys on the floor. Fantastic day!

Wednesday: Spent some time reading. We had our date night. It was great to see Miss Lori again (our sitter); she had been injured in a car accident and is better now. The boys were so excited that she was coming back. They were all asleep when we got home. Had a great dinner and got to talk for quite a while. Amazing day!

At the end of the week, create your story for the week, even if it is just in your head. Your story can only be written from positive events and things that are in your book. Skip the doctor's appointment, the lack of parking, the traffic problems, or even financial worries. Your story is about the great week you have had!

I had an UNBELIEVABLE week! I spent a lot of time with my family, made great strides in writing my book. It was a great success!

THAT is what I want in my memory bank!

People ask me how I can be so positive all of the time. My memory bank is full of positive Success Experiences. It does not happen on autopilot until you accumulate a longer list of Success Experience memories than non-success experience memories. With a little effort, you can do it too. Life is fun!

Success wall

Pictures of past Success Experiences help me to remember and relive the experience. On those rare occasions when I have a bad day, these pictures remind me of my blessings. Our favorite vacations, pictures of my family, a picture of my sky-diving experience, and running the mini-marathon. These pictures cover an entire wall in my office.

People naturally do this as they age. They surround themselves with little pictures of their loved ones, refrigerator magnets, and knick-knacks from their vacations. I use 8x10 or larger pictures. The pictures bring me back and let me relive the experience easily. I can get any picture blown up to that size for 5 bucks. These pictures help me when I get down on myself and motivate me to keep growing.

Your Success Experience

Love The Life You Live, Experience Your Success!

Patrick R. Lowe, D.C.

It's the LAW!

Recognition, appreciation, and approval

Reality shows are very popular right now: regular people doing irregular things. Many of these shows recruit volunteers to compete for promise large amounts of money for the winners. People will perform crazy stunts and eat everything from dead rats to rotten fish.

Yes, they have a chance at "big money". They were guaranteed to be on television, to have their friends, family, and neighbors watch them be a celebrity. When they were kicked off, they rarely complained about not winning the money. They mostly complain, "I wanted to be the _XYZ_ *Show* champion."

They receive recognition, appreciation, and approval. They receive the recognition of friends and family for being on television. Their claim to fame: "I was on _XYZ Show_!" I am certain that contestants recorded their own episode. Most people want to be famous. They receive appreciation for their contribution to "quality television", they receive approval for winning the prize. Winning the title of "Champion" provides added recognition, increases the appreciation from friends and family, and bumps their approval rating.

Encouragers use this principle to help other people reach their goals. They recognize accomplishments, appreciate people for their contribution and, and approve of people for who they are.

Chapter 8

Compound Interest of your Success Experiences

Understanding that Success is an Experience and understanding the psychology of change will help you achieve more of your big Success Experiences. Remember, "Knowledge *in action* is Power." The information in this book and any book is learned when it is read repetitively, three or more times.

Kaizen, small daily improvements, provides huge returns through the principle of compound interest. If you invested $1 and earned 2% interest every day, your money would double every 34 days. Because of the benefits of compound interest, that $1 would generate well over $1,904 in a year. At the same rate, it would generate over $3,608,000 in only two years.

Your Success Experience

Love The Life You Live, Experience Your Success!

Patrick R. Lowe, D.C.

Kaizen provides compound interest in our lives. Two percent improvement is accomplished with very little time and effort.

To achieve 2% interest:

- Read one book a month. You will have completed 12 books a year to help you grow.

- Meet with one personal mentor a week.

- Define your vision and cast it.

- Build your team.

- Make great deposits into your memory bank.

- Contribute to others.

> **"If you want something you've never had, you've got to do something you've never done."**
>
> Anonymous

In 5 years, you will not recognize the person you were when you started. What you have accomplished and become will be HUGE compared to what you are now. The Success Experiences you are dreaming about now will be a picture on your success wall. Your self-advertisement board will change, as you prepare for your next big Success Experience!

Your Success Experience

Love The Life You Live, Experience Your Success!

Patrick R. Lowe, D.C.

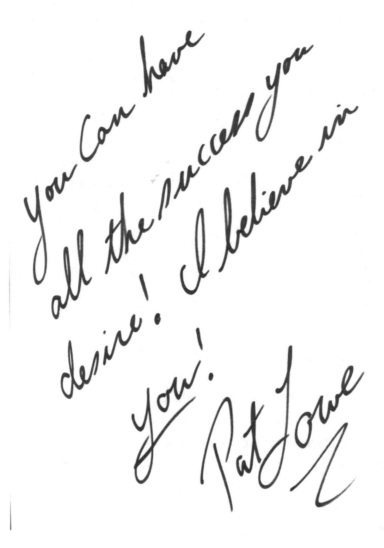

Notes

1. Harland Sanders Cafe and Museum. *www.corbinkentucky.us/sanderscafe.htm.* [Online] [Cited: July 27, 2007.] www.corbinkentucky.us/sanderscafe.

2. **Hopkins, A.D.** 1st100.com/part3/wynn.html. *1st 100* . [Online] Las Vegas Review-Journal, 2006. [Cited: August 9, 2006.] www.1st100.com.

3. **Hill, Napoleon.** *Think & Grow Rich 21st Century Edition.* Los Angeles CA : Highroads Media, 2004. Permission from Napleon Hill Foundations.

4. **Welch, Jack with John A Byrne.** *Jack, Straight from the Gut.* New York : Grand Central Publishing, 2001. 0-44-652838-2.

5. **Cathy, S. Truett.** *EAT MOR CHIKIN, INSPIRE MORE PEOPLE.* Decature : Looking Glass Books, 2002.

6. **Maxwell, John.** *Failing Forward.* Nashville TN : Thomas Nelson, 2000.

7. **Ziglar, Zig.** *Over the Top.* Nashville : Thomas Nelson, 1997. 978-0-7852-8877-0.

8. **Maxwell, John.** *New Leadership 101.* Tulsa, OK : Honor Books, 1997.

9. **Howard Gardner, Psychologist.** The Ethical Mind. *Harvard Business Review.* March 2007, Vol. 85, 3, p. 53.

10. **Kiyosaki, Robert.** *Rich Dad, Poor Dad.* New York : Grand Central Publishing, 1997 1998.

11. **Buford, Robert P.** *Halftime : Changing your game plan form success to significance.* Grand Rapids : Zondervan, 1994. 0-310-21532-3.

12. **Brown, Les.** Speak Your Way to Unlimited Wealth. *Speak Your Way to Unlimited Wealth.* [CD]

13. **Morgan, Jay.** *Gibson Management Seminar.* Astor Crowne Plaza, New Orleans , LA : Gibson Management Company, June 2006. Session 3.

14. **Eker, Harve.** *Secrets of the Millionaire Mind.* New York : HarperCollins, 2005. 0-06-076328-0.

15. **Martin, Roger.** How Successful Leaders Think. *Harvard Business Review.* June 2007, pp. 60-63.

16. **Haas Edersheim, Elizabeth.** *The Definitive Drucker.* New York : McGraw-Hill, 2007. pp. 224, 231-233. 10: 0-07-147233-9, 13:978-0-07-147233-3.

17. **Kuhn, Clifford M.D.** *THE FUN FACTOR.* Louisville : Minerva Books, LLC, 2002,2003. 0-9723992-5-9.